David Ingram's *15 Bedtime Stories* should find a place on the nightstands of entrepreneurial hopefuls everywhere. Each of his stories focuses on a key challenge faced by anyone starting a business. Ingram first describes what the challenge is and why it's important to address; his voice is clear, engaging, and authentic. Then he offers a bottom line takeaway—"the moral of the story"—followed by practical suggestions for reflection and action. Don't let the breeziness of his prose and the ease of reading fool you—this is a truly useful primer for navigating the wilds of new business creation.

—Erika Andersen,
Founder, Proteus International, Inc.;
Author, *Growing Great Employees* and *Being Strategic*

Better to learn from the experiences shared in *15 Bedtime Stories* than to learn the hard way—firsthand! Of the entrepreneurs we fund, those who succeed avoid most of the common mistakes because they can see them coming. This book can help you be prepared—because in any business you start, there are wrong turns at every intersection.

—John Backus,
Founder and Managing Partner, New Atlantic Ventures

15 Bedtime Stories That Keep Entrepreneurs Awake at Night is a must-read for everyone interested in starting a business. David Ingram is living proof that if you can dream it, you can do it, and he did it well.

—Hugh F. Gouldthorpe,
Senior Vice President, Owens & Minor;
Head Cheerleader, Quality and Communications;
Author, *I've Always Looked Up to Giraffes*

The book is very captivating and well-written. Each chapter reveals a little more about the man behind the company, which is a story in itself. I find myself wanting to read more from and about David Ingram!

—Tim Burress,
Cofounder and President, Cohesive Knowledge Solutions, Inc.;
Co-author, *The Hamster Revolution*

David Ingram's book is a fantastic read. It is essentially fifteen stories that cover common sense and a few unexpected ideas on starting and running a world-class business. Entrepreneurs need to know how to lead a firm and avoid the truly damaging pitfalls that lead to failure. David's stories can save a CEO a lot of heartache.

—David R. Barrett,
Founder and CEO, Barrett Capital Management, LLC;
Past Chairman, Virginia Council of CEOs

15 Bedtime Stories contains a wealth of experience that entrepreneurs, potential entrepreneurs, and entrepreneurship students will find interesting and helpful. It describes real challenges faced by most entrepreneurs at some time or other. As such, it is valuable as a tool to help anticipate problems and determine how to prevent or resolve them before they become serious. The book is especially relevant to entrepreneurs in service businesses, although any entrepreneur will benefit from reading it.

—Dr. Jeff Harrison,
The W. David Robbins Chair in Strategic Management;
Robins School of Business,
University of Richmond

I literally could not put it down. I think it was because I could relate so much to many of the situations David described. I could feel tension building in myself as I read the accounts of various financial and personnel crises. But after each chapter, I found myself too tempted to read one more to stop until I had finished the whole book. David's book does a phenomenal job of recreating his incredible life story—and just barely comes up short of being there with him as things happened.

—Steve Barley,
CEO, Lawyer's Staffing+Medicus Staffing

Terrific common sense served in bite-sized digestible portions full of the right vitamins and minerals for a healthy growing business—well done.

—Doug Tatum,
Chairman Emeritus, Tatum LLC; Author, *No Man's Land*

The principles and lessons discussed in *15 Bedtime Stories That Keep Entrepreneurs Awake at Night* can be applied to many different business settings, so I added it to the reading list for all my graduate and undergraduate management classes.

—W. Lee Grubb III, Ph.D.,
Associate Professor of Management,
East Carolina University

W. Somerset Maugham was asked the secret to writing a great novel. He said, "There's got to be a man behind the book." A few pages into the introduction to *15 Bedtime Stories That Keep Entrepreneurs Awake at Night*, you know there's a man of integrity behind this book. What a pleasure to read such clear, straightforward writing (no gimmicks or jargon) that communicates much-needed insights in a unique and interesting way. More importantly, there is a humanity here—a commitment to serve—that is rare and oh-so-welcome. David Ingram shows how to run an entrepreneurial business that makes a positive, profitable difference for all involved. Read it and reap.

—Sam Horn,
Communications Consultant;
Author, *POP! Stand Out in Any Crowd*

I know how on-target David's stories are because I have experienced many of them as an entrepreneur myself. David puts himself and his experience right out there for all to see and benefit from. I believe everyone that reads this will appreciate the candor, humor, and emotion that are right out there on the page for all to absorb.

—Tom Ficklin,
President, White Oak Equipment

This is not really a book. It is a conversation with the author. It is also a lesson in life that gives the reader hope. It is not an exposé written tabloid-style, but it is filled with brutal honesty. It is also a wake-up call, but different from most because of the emotions demonstrated in each chapter. I really got the feeling that the author has walked in my shoes.

—Ted R. Abernathy, M.D. FAAP,
Pediatric and Adolescent Health Partners, P.C.

Regardless of what industry you are in, or what type of company you are looking to start, *15 Bedtime Stories* will help highlight issues and pitfalls that any entrepreneur should be aware of before embarking on his journey.

—Colin Day,
Founder and CEO, iCIMS;
2007 Ernst & Young Entrepreneur of the Year—Information Technology Software category

The kind of wisdom imparted here can only be gained in the trials of experience. Read this book to avoid some of the most common traps for entrepreneurs.

—Keith McFarland,
#1 Best-selling Author, *The Breakthrough Company* and *Bounce*

This is an entrepreneurial lesson book where you feel as if you are sitting across the table and talking with the teacher. It is an easy read with powerful examples to improve your business skills.

—Jack Stack,
President and CEO, SRC Holdings Corporation;
Co-author, *The Great Game of Business*

I wish I'd had this book when I started my first company. The bedtime story format is awesome—presenting many important lessons for first-time entrepreneurs in an easy-to-consume format.

—Brad Feld,
Managing Director, Foundry Group

Having personally worked with over fifteen thousand entrepreneurs since 1991, I can tell you that every one of the fifteen bedtime stories contains a lesson that a budding entrepreneur needs to learn.

—Mo Fathelbab,
President, Forum Resources Network;
Author, *FORUM: The Secret Advantage of Successful Leaders*

15 BEDTIME STORIES

That Keep Entrepreneurs Awake at Night

15 BEDTIME STORIES

That Keep Entrepreneurs Awake at Night

DAVID INGRAM

HigherLife

DEVELOPMENT SERVICES

Orlando, Florida

15 Bedtime Stories That Keep Entrepreneurs Awake at Night
by David Ingram

Published by HigherLife Development Services, Inc.
2342 Westminster Terrace
Oviedo, Florida 32765
(407) 563-4806
www.ahigherlife.com

Disclaimer: The stories and information in this book represent my personal experiences. They are intended to educate and do not claim to provide professional advice. Please seek the counsel of appropriate professionals before acting in any issues that may arise. Some of the details, names, facts, and stories have been changed to maintain the flow of the book. The experiences, advice, and strategies contained in this book may not be appropriate for your organization and you should consult a professional for individual guidance.

ISBN: 978-1-935245-03-2

Cover Illustrator: Doug Thompson

Cover Design: Eric Powell

First Edition

09 10 11 12 13 — 8 7 6 5 4 3 2 1

Printed in the United States of America

DEDICATION

*To my wife Meridith, without whom this book
never would have been started... or finished.*

TABLE OF CONTENTS

LETTER FROM DAVID

I REMEMBER SITTING WITH MY HEAD held in my hands a number of years ago, unsure if my fledgling business was going to survive. We had lost our largest client and had a significant cash flow problem. I wasn't really considering bankruptcy at that point, but I was petrified by the thought of failing—both personally and professionally—and losing everything I had worked so hard to build over the years. I lost a lot of sleep.

Fast forward to 2009. We have grown fast enough to win Inc. 5000 recognition the past two years in a row as one of the country's fastest-growing private companies. Earning Inc. 5000 recognition has been incredibly valuable to us. Not only was the award recognition of superior performance, but it opened doors to excellent resources through the Inc. Web site, as well as the incredibly motivating and educational conferences and seminars. We are surviving one of the worst economies I can remember. We are making it. When I was in such a bad spot several years ago, I wish that I had a book like this one to reassure me and help me stave off insomnia.

I hope you find insight and empathy in these pages. The stories start with issues that you may face in the early stages of your business, and gradually progress to more complex situations that may arise as your company becomes more established. Each chapter begins with a real-life story that either I, or someone I know, has been through. I then discuss the outcome and what was learned in the process—in other words, "the moral of the story." At the end of each chapter, I pose basic questions that I wish someone had asked me at that point of my own entrepreneurial journey. I hope they inspire contemplation and action to help you avoid some of the mistakes I've made.

I do not provide specific solutions for the problems that you may face. But I do hope you will find your way to your own solutions, educated by these real-life experiences and secure in the knowledge that there are other people out there facing similar challenges.

There are many individuals I owe a debt of gratitude for their support and inspiration—my family, my advisors, my clients, you, my fellow entrepreneurs, and also my coworkers (without whom the company would not thrive), who are a positive force for our company as well as the community. I hope that you enjoy these stories.

Sweet dreams,

David

If you enjoyed this letter and would like to read more, visit David's blog at http://www.15bedtimestories.com.

Introduction
Once Upon a Time

Why Bedtime Stories?

Who doesn't love a good bedtime story? The simple phrase "Once upon a time" can transport us back to childhood—when Mom or Dad read aloud to us, or when we hid under the covers with a flashlight to read until our eyelids grew heavy and we drifted off to sleep. But bedtime stories aren't just for children. They come in many forms—fables, fairy tales, novels, poetry, Scripture, and even tales from the trenches told by successful CEOs. They can inspire, teach, and frighten.

Too often for business leaders—especially entrepreneurs—bedtime reading has the latter effect. The stories are scary. They keep us awake at night wondering if the "boogeyman" is hiding in the closet or under the bed. In this book, I've compiled some "bedtime stories" of my own, pulling together some of my experiences as well as tales from other entrepreneurs I know. My hope is that you won't lie awake at night wondering how you will survive the inevitable turbulence of starting and growing a company, but will sleep easy in the knowledge that others have successfully navigated the same waters.

The Best Time to Make Your Move

My story—at least the chapter I'm in right now—began in 2001. I had had enough of what was, for me, a grinding corporate existence, and I was ready to set out on my own. My timing wasn't stellar—the economic environment was as uncertain then as it is as I write this book in the second half of 2008 and the first half of

2009. You may think that there couldn't be a worse time to start something new than today: Banks are going under, stalwarts of our economy such as Fannie Mae and Freddie Mac are reeling, and the stock market has proven to be as fickle and capricious as the Beanie Babies market, even for visionaries like Warren Buffett.

When my journey as an entrepreneur began in 2001, the mood wasn't very different. It felt as though our country's economy might be as vulnerable as the Twin Towers. The Internet "bubble" was popping, and the tech stocks that gave the thirty-something generation such a heady start in the business world were in free fall. Most people probably thought it was a strange (and unwise) time to say, "Hey! Let's start a business!" My wife and I did it anyway.

We unlocked our HELOC (home equity line of credit) and saddled up, along with our newborn twins, and we were off to the races! Hint: Just as there will never be a perfect time to have kids, there will never be a perfect time to become an entrepreneur. If you think waiting will provide you with better starting conditions for following such a dream, you'll be waiting for the rest of your working days.

Ironically, my own entrepreneurial adventure began out of a sense of risk aversion. I know that sounds crazy, but I had a burning desire to control my own destiny by creating my own job—something that would support my family. Depending upon my own efforts felt less risky than depending upon the efforts of an impersonal company.

I had spent the previous fifteen years working for some amazing companies. The background of outstanding training and great bosses were big factors in giving me the confidence to hang out my own shingle. Maybe even more importantly, I had watched my father start something from scratch, build it successfully through many trials and tribulations, earn awards, and then prosper from an eventual buyout. I had spent my career fighting fires, building sales organizations, achieving challenging objectives, and climbing seemingly insurmountable mountains— all for other people's companies. How hard could it be to do it for myself?

There were other reasons, too. My wife and I had moved six times in seven years, which takes a toll on relationship building and becomes less feasible with kids. Sure, my willingness to relocate and to accept new responsibilities meant making lots of money, but when it came right down to it, not only were the constant moves wearing us out, but my own goals and desires were being neglected. Selfishly, I decided that I was sick of building great teams for the benefit of someone else. Plus, truth be told, I was pretty burned out from the pace I was keeping. I needed some extra time to pick up the sticks and play golf, run a marathon, and sleep late to make up for hours I lost when the twins first came home from the hospital.

So I started a small executive search firm, where I could work the hours I wanted, for the clients I wanted, making good money and getting a great overall view of the marketplace—enabling me to plot my next move. During this time, I also hoped to recharge my batteries and get my enthusiasm level back up. But after just three weeks of that kind of lifestyle, I experienced the reverse of what I hoped would happen: I found myself becoming depressed. Sure, I could go to the office and make enough money to pay my bills, but I lacked any real sense of fulfillment. Work was not inspiring greatness in me—it had become a grind again.

Just One More Move

After three years of establishing roots in a lovely section of north-west Washington, D.C., our twins were growing and we faced the prospect of putting them in a private school. The thought was daunting, to say the least. My wife, Meridith, and I decided that it might be time to move. Three years was, in fact, the longest we had lived anywhere. We considered the suburbs; I suggested

Great Falls, but my lovely bride asked with a shrug, "Really, how much more difficult could it be to move back to Richmond?" We lived there briefly right after our marriage and loved it for the quality of life—low costs, great schools, and very little traffic. After all, she pointed out, I only needed a telephone and an airport to operate my boutique executive search firm, right? So we cashed out of a vibrant D.C. real estate market, hoping to downsize, cut costs, and live the good life for a few years until I decided what I wanted to be when I grew up.

I shouldn't have been surprised to discover that I was soon doing the same thing in a different place; my business life was, in a word, boring. I don't mean to complain; I was blessed with success. I just had a deep sense there was something more I could achieve.

If I've learned one thing about myself, it's that I prefer to be a starter, not a maintainer. I like to swoop in, fix, reorient, and then swoop back out. My wife calls me "Mr. Fix-It" whenever she starts a conversation and I try to end it with a quick solution. It's true. I like to fix things. And I do not have much experience—or desire—with running anything in a static state for a long period of time. I have a low threshold for inertia, which may resonate with a lot of you entrepreneurs out there.

Standing at this crossroads, my wife and I decided to double-down financially, delay our long cherished dream of a vacation house, and invest more deeply in the business. I wanted to build something that was really special, something I could look back on with pride and satisfaction. I wanted to surround myself with great people and provide an opportunity for them to achieve their personal goals and enjoy ownership of their own successes. I wanted to build a culture in which working hard and having fun went hand-in-hand, a place where you'd just as likely find a dart-board as a whiteboard.

I was also in search of a business model that created true wealth, not just a W-2 for me and the people who helped me get there. I wanted to build a platform where I didn't need to be present for success to happen. At one point, I wanted to create a new business, or a line of businesses within our current model, every six months. In that phase, I didn't mind taking risks because I felt as though I had the credentials to fall back into the corporate world if I ever needed to. Again, it's just not my style to sit back and enjoy the ride.

Only One Viable Option

At one point I realized I had created something in which I was so financially involved that I had no option but to succeed. I had sixty people who worked for me, plus their families, for whom I now felt responsible—not just my own wife and children. Moreover, we supported organizations that depended on us—children's causes that truly benefited from our contributions. In fact, over the previous three years, we had given in excess of 7.5 percent of our net income back to the community. I felt like those organizations needed us, that there was a greater good at stake in my business life, not just the money in my own pocket.

In order to meet these goals and satisfy the criteria for satisfaction and success, I needed to create a repeatable process, focus on a different type of customer than I had in the past, generate enough cash flow to pay the bills, and prepare an eventual exit strategy. Spelled out on paper, that might sound easy, but I have found that the difference between the utopian idea of "starting your own business" and the reality of actually doing so can be pretty painful. Throughout the past eight years, I have run into some really crazy situations and spent many sleepless nights pondering what I thought were unusually challenging situations.

My nocturnal problem solving usually takes place from 3 to 4 A.M. several times a week; many of you may have similar sleep-robbing sessions. Given what we have on the line, I am not surprised—or even upset, really—by this pattern of sleeplessness.

I've come to realize that true entrepreneurs, the ones who risk their personal livelihood—and their family's—to chase a dream, expose themselves to extraordinary situations and have to adopt a different decision-making perspective than those who "play with someone else's money." It's the nature of owning a business. Questions such as, "Do I open a new office this year or send my children to private schools?" or "Do I hire additional salespeople or start doubling my IRA contributions?" are far more complex than they were when my paycheck came from an outside corporation. The answers are intertwined with many more factors.

I have also learned that I can't be surprised anymore by anything that comes across my path. After all, the bigger the company, the more people we work with, the more exposure to situations of the odd, fantastic, truth-is-stranger-than-fiction variety. Business owners will encounter challenging situations, large and small, mundane and fantastic, and may even lose a little sleep in the process. For me, the key to getting the forty winks I so desperately need is to know that anything we've been through as a company can only make us stronger, as long as we go about solving our challenges with the right processes, standards, and ethics.

The Big Picture

Maybe the risk factor is still what's holding you back. But just look around you at today's business climate—how safe is corporate life these days? Are you satisfied to put your future success into the hands of someone else whose primary responsibility is not your welfare?

With some determination and even just a small dose of courage, you have what it takes to follow your dreams of building a sustainable business. I believe that when people risk their personal livelihoods to chase a dream and make a difference, they can and will find incredible levels of success and fulfillment. And

I believe that entrepreneurs and small businesses are going to be the catalyst for helping us recover from this woeful economy.

I can't cover all the dynamics that go into starting a new business in this slim volume, but I will hit upon the relevant issues—early stage, mid-stage, and then some of the later-stage dynamics that you will face as you build your business. You will learn invaluable lessons from the experiences of real entrepreneurs, with a very frank look at the challenges that you will encounter along the way.

My goal with this book is not to share my insomnia with readers. Although my "bedtime stories" tell of frightening business challenges, for the most part, each has a happy ending. As you go through each chapter, I would encourage you to really interact with the material—even if you disagree with me on a few points—by working through the questions for reflection and action at the end of each chapter. The process may help resolve—or, better yet, prevent—problems in your own business. I also recommend you keep a bedside journal to put the answers down on paper so they don't bounce around in your head, keeping you awake all night.

I don't expect you to relate to all aspects of my story, nor do I believe that everything I've done has universal application, but I hope you will find both inspiration and information in these pages. This particular chapter of my journey has a happy ending. My firm's revenues have grown 436 percent since 2004, earning us a spot on the prestigious Inc. 5000 list of The Fastest-Growing Private Companies in America (http://www.inc.com/inc5000/). We are a long way away from our "once upon a time" in 2001.

A year, or even ten years from now, when you tell the story of your own entrepreneurial journey to friends, like many grand stories, it too will begin... "Once upon a time."

Chapter 1

DON'T RUN OUT OF CASH

Revenue is vanity. Margin is sanity. Cash is king.

—Anonymous

IN MY FIRST DAYS AS an entrepreneur, I didn't see any risk in the venture I was starting because I had solid credentials in software sales management. The year before I took the plunge, I had done well, earned bonuses, and saved some money. I figured I had succeeded in a competitive corporate environment, so I could do it again on my own. And if things didn't work out, I could always hop back into corporate life at any time (or so I thought).

To fund my new venture, I had some conversations with small angel venture* people, all of who were very gracious with their time. They told me, in a nutshell, that given the stage I was in, the nature of the business itself, and my experience, any startup money I needed would have to come from friends and family, or I would have to supply it myself—in other words, the bootstrap model. Frankly, I agreed with them. Mentally, I wasn't wholly committed to the idea of running a business yet. I was looking for a place to land on my feet, make a little money, and see what happened. I didn't want to take on a load of debt.

---

* An angel specializes in funding small startups, with terms that include premium interest rates or a stake in the company. Since banks have traditionally not been as risk tolerant, the premium pays for the inventor's risk level.

I decided to self-fund and identified my two cash reserves. One consisted of what I was comfortable risking, which included the equity in my house, accessed through my HELOC. The second was an emergency fund—all of the shekels I had managed to sock away over the years. I believed fund number one provided about six months' operating expenses. Naïve. I would soon learn that everything a new business needs to get started is three times more expensive than anticipated. And if that isn't enough to mess up cash flow projections, I would also learn that everything takes longer to develop than you planned—especially receiving payments from clients.

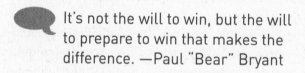

It's not the will to win, but the will to prepare to win that makes the difference. —Paul "Bear" Bryant

During my planning period, one of my advisors had asked to see a copy of my financial statement. I handed her a one-page hand-drawn chart, and I told her she was looking at it. As far as I was concerned, it was simple: me, one employee, cash in, cash out. All my projections started low and left and went up and right. Who plans for a business to go down? I had no clue how company financial statements really worked. I felt as though I could figure out just about anything on the back of a napkin, so I wasn't concerned. I thought to myself, *How hard could this be? It's simple addition and subtraction.* Compared to working for a publicly traded software company—where it was understood that if you missed your quarterly goals, you were fired—this would be a breeze. In fact, in some ways, ignorance was bliss to me at that point. I didn't feel like making a business plan; it seemed like a waste of time. I just needed clients and placements and did not want to divert from that focus.

You Can Always Count on Bills Coming In

My business was exclusively in the field of executive search at the time. I would find clients that needed people and people that needed work. I landed a few assignments from previous contacts with companies that had openings in Boston, Washington, D.C., and San Francisco. I started my day working on connections for the East Coast and worked my way west. I knew that if I made a minimum of 100 outbound calls a day, I would be successful. I'm not sure why I picked 100. It was a nice, round number, and realistically, I could make calls to the West Coast until nine or ten o'clock at night. It made for a long day, but I was used to long days and expected to add significant quantities of sweat equity to building a successful venture. This was actually a bit easier than my former corporate life, which was filled with interruptions and external pressures. As a bonus, there was a gym in the building, so I could sneak in a workout at lunch or in late afternoon.

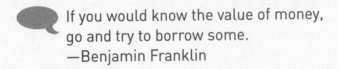

If you would know the value of money,
go and try to borrow some.
—Benjamin Franklin

I realize now that the rush of doing my own thing crowded any kind of sane financial rationale out of my mind. I had figured out how much I had in the bank and HELOC, subtracted rent, salary for my coworker, business expenses, and my own living expenses, and divided the number out to see how many months I could float with no income. Okay, I didn't have the six months of cash I originally projected, but I still had a four-month head start. I was fine with that—at least until the bills started piling up with no money coming in on schedule. I had not internalized the concept of cash flow, especially the time gap between selling something and getting paid. My four-month supply of cash was soon down to three months.

My father, who is one of my closest advisors, used to tell me, "David, you can always count on the bills coming in. You can't always count on money coming in." How right he was. I didn't realize how little I understood the concept of cash flow until I was several months into the business. If I sound repetitious...good. It bears repeating. In most businesses, there is a difficult time period between fulfilling a contract and getting paid. What if I had enough money for thirty days, but placed someone on sixty-day terms? Whoops. Time to dip into emergency reserves. Now I was digging deeper and more often into my reserves than I dreamed possible in my worst-case scenario on the back of a napkin. The reality of not having enough money for my fourth month of payroll and rent, much less future investments, had never occurred to me. Now it was becoming a distinct possibility.

You Can Be Profitable—and Broke

I'm still not a big advocate of elaborate and long-winded business plans, but you do need a real financial model, one that shows profits and losses—and cash flows. Without the cash flow chart, you can find yourself thinking you're highly profitable—with P&Ls to prove it—only to wake up broke. I eventually hired a talented person to take the simple chart I created and turn it into a robust model that included payout and pay-in assumptions. These turned into extensive spreadsheets that all linked in ways I will never really understand—and don't intend to. The result was a financial dashboard—an interactive front-page summary sheet—based on my key performance indicators. This dashboard helped me see around financial corners. It allowed me to run "what-if" scenarios to determine how and when investments would pay off in the future, and it showed me the real interdependencies of the different components of my business. I was able to focus my efforts and my investments on activities that improved my company's performance. But most of all, as a start-up entrepreneur, I had a tool that allowed me to keep the lights turned on, my employee paid, and my door open.

Your First Hire

I had no clue what I was doing when I hired my first employee and really anguished over the decision. The main reason I struggled so much was I was evaluating the decision to hire strictly on the basis of how much it was going to cost me. The real question was, What would the net result be, using a cost-benefit model? How much was this person going to add to my company through his own sales efforts or by relieving me of tasks so I could concentrate on making more sales? My answer was much easier than I made it.

Sit down with your accountant and treat the decision to hire the same way you would decide whether to purchase a new piece of equipment or software application.

Bottom line: First-year companies make it or break it on the basis of cash flow, not a profit-and-loss sheet. Both are important, but make sure you have enough cash to succeed.

Invest in a Financial Expert

The old adage is that every business needs a good lawyer and a good banker. I also think you need an expert financial planner up front, someone who will help you see the real costs of doing business on a month-to-month basis.

Financial modeling may not be your forte, but you can find someone who can take your draft financial plan and create a usable compass for making sound financial decisions. Proceeding without expert advice is like buying an elaborate swing set and putting it together without instructions. You may feel like you're starting fine, but it will take a whole lot longer to undo your mistakes—and you may be putting those kids who will sit in the swings or zoom down the slide, in danger. You can't afford the time you will lose working and reworking financial models because in business, time is money.

Your financial analyst may actually be a commercial software program. That's fine. There are some excellent tools available that are affordable and user-friendly. But if you go this route, make sure you learn how to use what you buy. Don't be like the person who buys a Mercedes and drives it like he is sitting behind the wheel of a beat-up 1974 Pinto. You'll probably need to hire a living, breathing financial expert to at least teach you how to drive and give you a road map to success.

You can easily set up your first-year cash flow using Microsoft Excel or another spreadsheet program. This may look much different from your monthly P&L: If you don't have the cash and grow faster than your spending speed limit, you can easily go out of business by being too successful. The keys to building this successfully are to:

- Make sure you have gathered all your expenses and revenues. If you feel like you're forgetting something, pad the expenses.

- Make sure you assign expenses and revenues to the months when they will hit—don't forget that in a tough economy, your customers may be paying slower than promised and your vendors will be pressing for payment.

- Run a simple addition and subtraction formula that carries over the balance to your next month's line.

- Make sure your bottom number stays in the black or make sure you have a plan for those months it goes in the red—a line of credit, a family member angel, less salary for you, etc.

The rule of thumb is to build your first set of expenses—and then add significant padding. Even if exact projections are impossible to achieve, the harder you work at this, the closer you will come to an accurate cash flow—and the more sanity you will have in your life. You really do need to learn the performance metrics that will indicate success or failure for your enterprise. Knowing your true profits and losses in the context of a positive balance sheet, having the ability to ask "what if" questions for time and money decisions, and comparing the returns on different investment scenarios is worth the time, energy, and money you spend up front.

Lord Alfred Tennyson's most famous poem, *The Charge of the Light Brigade,* contains these haunting lines:

> *Theirs not to make reply,*
> *Theirs not to reason why,*
> *Theirs but to do and die*

This classic bedtime reading is based on a true event from the Crimean War, where Lord Cardigan led a regiment of more than six hundred British cavalrymen on a reckless and foolish charge into a massive Russian artillery position. Only a third of the men survived unscathed. Tennyson wrote this narrative to extol the glory of courage and duty—but also to warn of the folly of the kind of daring that rushes blindly into conflict. Not even enthusiasm can overcome fundamental miscalculations.

When Cash Gets Tight

1. Can you pay yourself less on a temporary basis? Many start-ups fail because owners take out too much money for themselves in the early days.

2. Contact your vendors and ask for an extension of terms. Take the initiative if you want to keep them working for you!

3. Can you trade some margin for faster payment terms with some of your key customers? I don't like this approach, because even if offered as a temporary measure, the customer may resume slower payments but never agree to the previous margin levels.

4. Have you been in business long enough to establish a new or additional line of credit?

This chapter is not intended to give you an excuse to climb down from the horse and return to a "safer" status quo. But it is a reminder that successful entrepreneurs count the costs of any venture—all the costs!

The Moral of the Story

Don't run out of cash. Revenue arrives slower and costs come in faster and higher than planned. I thought I knew this—and inherently I did—but I didn't truly *understand* it until I had to make payroll one Friday by writing a personal check because my company cash well was dry. Create contingencies far beyond what you think you will need.

For Reflection and Action

1. How detailed are your financial projections? Do you know how long your cash reserves will last if you have a bad quarter?

2. How much risk are you willing to take? Don't forget intangible costs as well as tangible ones.

3. Have you made realistic plans for raising extra cash if something unexpected happens? Whom are you willing to go to, and how will you compensate them?

4. A wise man said that one way companies go out of business is by being too successful. (The culprit is cash flow.) Does this scenario possibly apply to you?

5. Are you able to keep an eye on your profit and losses both today and three months down the road?

Chapter 2

Don't Ignore Trusted Advisors

Many receive advice, only the wise profit from it.

—Publilius Syrus

EVERAL YEARS AGO, I REALIZED I needed some structured oversight. My business was growing, and the impact of my decisions was growing in proportion. The bottom line began to include numbers larger than anything I could solve with a simple draw-from-my-home credit line. We were making multi-year, substantial commitments with long-term implications that needed careful consideration. From a planning standpoint, I was venturing into uncharted territory. This was bigger than anything I had previously done. I was worried that I might be losing objectivity in some of my long-range decision making. Though these are typically good problems for an entrepreneur to have, I knew I needed a reality—and sanity—check.

I eventually came up with the notion that I needed to create an advisory board. While I had, and continue to have, plenty of "advisors" that I interact with on an informal basis—fellow business owners I can meet for lunch, go for a run with, or attend a professional seminar with—I felt that I needed a separate, objective group. (See chapter 4 for more on informal advisors and feedback.)

A board can mean many different things to different organizations, and a board can serve a wide variety of purposes— introducing you to new accounts, generating buzz, making valuable connections, and the list goes on. But I wasn't interested in meeting any of those particular objectives by creating a board. I was interested in a group of people who were interested in me and my business, who had a track record of success in their own endeavors. I wanted people who could focus on David Ingram, with all his strengths and weaknesses, and who would affirm me in my best decisions and stand up to me when I was off in the weeds. I wanted a board of experienced executives—not stockholders, not potential clients—with whom I had a personal relationship, who could look at numbers without bias, see around corners at what might loom ahead, and help make sure I was leading my company in the right direction for growth and prosperity. I needed people who could be unfailingly objective in their guidance.

I found three such experienced, interested people, and they all accepted my offer. I paid them for their time. The amount was trivial to them at this point in their lives, but for me it was a significant investment and added import to that four-hour meeting once a quarter. It showed them that I was serious and that I valued every minute of their time—and expected them to provide me with valuable input.

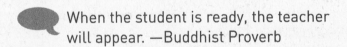 When the student is ready, the teacher will appear. —Buddhist Proverb

While I didn't report to this board and I had no fiduciary responsibility to them, I did prepare a series of reports each quarter—key performance indicators, strategic development ideas, and other documents to honestly reflect what was happening in my business. I also presented the three biggest challenges currently facing the company, along with three proposed solutions. I asked, "Based on what you're seeing in these reports, do you think these are, in fact, our biggest challenges? What am

I missing? If I'm on target, what do you think of my solutions?" Sometimes I would leave the meeting having been right on; other times, the analysis and discourse revealed entirely different areas that needed attention.

How important were they to me as a start-up entrepreneur? I still meet with them every quarter. This advisory board still provides a great system of checks and balances. But, as I learned the hard way, it only works if you actually *listen*.

Plans to Expand—Go West, Young Man!

At one of our quarterly meetings several years ago, we discussed expanding the company. We were getting into a mode where we were *really* making progress. Our people were successful. Our confidence was high. I felt as though we had created a repeatable business process; in fact, we had a patent pending on our methodology. It was truly special, different, and ours. We knew our model was really working and that we were absolutely in our element. So after consulting with my key managers, I proposed to my advisory board that we replicate this model of success in another market. That's what successful companies do, right? Expand!

I made my pitch with great enthusiasm—and it was met with the sound of crickets. They shuffled papers, asked me a few questions, shared a few comments in measured tones, and tossed out some vague suggestions. You get the picture. To say the least, they didn't jump on the table and shout, "Eureka! Do it!"

Maybe they were testing me, I thought, because they didn't come right out and say *don't do it*, but they certainly didn't encourage it. I took it as their "blessing" when I saw more smiles than frowns as we determined approximate costs of the expansion scrawling some crude metrics on a whiteboard. In effect, it would be a pretty inexpensive experiment—or so I thought. Like the ever-building entrepreneurs and undefeatable people that I believed myself and my people to be, we opened another location just a few hours away from our home office.

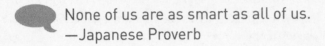

None of us are as smart as all of us.
—Japanese Proverb

About a year into the endeavor, that office was doing okay. Not great, not terrible, just okay. It wasn't exploding, it wasn't bleeding cash, but it was draining a great amount of energy (mine) and resources (mine) from the home office. It was absolutely not proving to be a duplicate model of what we were accomplishing in the home office. We were beginning to realize that this satellite had the potential to bring down the mother ship, which wasn't doing quite so well itself due to a lack of attention. At another advisory board meeting, we determined that the office structure was all wrong—the wrong people were doing the wrong jobs—it was just all wrong. We had to reorganize our efforts.

Long story short, it became clear that we needed to proceed in a different way, so the next day I drove to that office and gave everyone the bad news. I was reorganizing our company, and that office didn't fit our overall strategy. Ouch. It was not one of the most pleasant days of my life; in fact, in many respects, it was one of the hardest days I've experienced personally or professionally. But mentally, financially, and in the best interest of our employees there and at the home office, it was the right thing to do.

Just as a quick aside, it wasn't the people in that office's fault for getting laid off. It was clearly mine. I had lost sight of the overall mission, and had been trying to expand without the right strategy or people in place to make it successful. On my way out of the board meeting when it was affirmed I needed to close the branch, one of the members looked at me and chuckled woefully, recalling the meeting a year earlier, during which this same group of trusted advisors had asked me probing, pointed questions—questions that I did not want to answer truthfully. I had my blinders on and saw and heard only what worked for my agenda. My advisor didn't come out and say, "I told you so," but he should have!

The Experience of Others Pays Off

There are always going to be people out there who have more experience than you do. A lot more experience. Befriend them, pay them, do what you have to do to benefit from their knowledge. It will pay off in dividends.

Where do you start? Look for advisors who:

- Know you well enough to have a good sense of both your strengths and your weaknesses;

- Know how to disagree and question without discord and rancor—yes, you need an objective point of view, but you don't need an unnecessary battleground;

- Know how your business—or similar kinds of businesses—function and succeed.

One great resource that you might want to turn to first is called SCORE (www.score.org), which is an organization made up of successful entrepreneurs and executives—many retired—who volunteer to mentor individuals as they start new businesses and run small companies. How much does it cost? Only your time. It's a nonprofit organization that provides you with this service at no cost.

Being an entrepreneur and small-business owner is heady stuff. Indeed, the risks and challenges are great. But you don't need to weather those storms alone. Even when the sun is shining on your business, you can always stand to have an honest, reliable, consistent system of checks and balances behind you. In fact, I'd argue that you have to be even more cautious and more open to advice during good times. Why? To keep your ego in check and not allow excitement to color black-and-white reality. There's nothing wrong with enjoying growth and success, as long as your enthusiasm doesn't take over the most necessary aspect of being a CEO: objectivity where the bottom line is concerned.

I'm sure you've experienced something like this: Someone comes to you complaining, perhaps asking for advice. You give him some. He doesn't listen. He comes back to you later with the same challenge and problem. You repeat your counsel. He doesn't listen. We all know those people. You may have been that person; maybe you still are that person. It's human nature. But after my lesson with a failed expansion, I learned that when my advisory board speaks, I listen. When they tell me something, I do it. If I don't agree, and if I believe it's wrong, we discuss the issue with the goal of finding common ground. At minimum, if I don't take the advice of my board, I do it with my eyes wide open. In other words, you and I can't afford to be that person who never listens.

How to Be a Good Mentee

- Cultivate both confidence and humility.
- Take the initiative to establish the relationship.
- Come prepared to meetings.
- Be open and honest—this is not about "selling" yourself.
- Question to understand—not to argue.
- Make a commitment to the relationship.

Is listening to an advisory board slower and more of a hassle sometimes? You bet. But it's worth it. Remember the bedtime story about the emperor who had no clothes? He was vain and subject to flattery—and his subjects were happy to oblige his vanity and tell him only what he wanted to hear. A sneaky con artist took advantage of the emperor's pride and promised to make him clothes out of a thread that was only visible to the wise. Like other promises that sound too good to be true, the thread was nothing more than hype and air. When the emperor appeared in public with his invisible clothes, only one young boy had the courage to stand up and say, "The king has no clothes!"

CEOs who listen to honest advisors never show up naked in public.

The Moral of the Story

Recruit—and heed—a trusted group of advisors who won't just say what you want to hear. A completely objective board is a necessity—but you have to be willing to listen to them.

For Reflection and Action

1. Do you have people in your life—not just in your business— who are honest and candid with you? If not, do you think you communicate, verbally or nonverbally, that you aren't going to listen?

2. If a reporter were to interview a family member, a neighbor, someone you know in a civic organization or at church, and a work colleague, what would the reporter hear from these sources about your willingness to listen?

3. Write the names of ten people from whom you would cherish receiving advice and counsel.

4. Before you go one step further in planning a new venture, put together a forum with at least three advisors to discuss and even challenge your ideas.

Chapter 3

Don't Lock Your Doors

Never cut what you can untie.

—Joseph Joubert

I F YOU WERE GIVEN A magic lamp with three wishes for your business, would you wish for great employees who would stay at your company forever? That would be *my* first wish. Every business owner knows that finding good employees can be one of the most frustrating, painful, and challenging parts of the job. Of course, we believe everyone should care as much as we do and be as selflessly dedicated to our companies as we are, but short of that pipe dream, we're ecstatic to find people we can trust to do their jobs well and get along with others. When we find these special individuals, we hope they'll never leave. So when they do, it can be hard to find a positive perspective, and even harder to find a replacement.

Let's face it. Even though there is something very appealing about working for a startup or young company—energy, growth, faster advancement, perhaps an equity stake—the support systems are usually not as established. This can be frustrating, and sometimes the pay is less than industry standards, even if there is the promise of more in the future. There will be turnover. How will you handle it? Will you write people off? Will you make counteroffers that don't make sense?

Check Your Ego Before You Burn Bridges

My business began as a fraternity of sorts, where everyone I hired was my buddy. Once I realized the importance of choosing people who actually fit a position and got over my inclination to hire only people I knew, I was fortunate to find some truly ideal employees for my company. The talented team we assembled was one of the main reasons that we experienced exponential growth right out of the starting gate, doubling and then quadrupling production from year to year. The office frenzy was palpable and contagious while the company exploded, but growth couldn't continue at that level forever. It's like a workout program. In the early days, when you are way out of shape, it's much easier to lose weight and experience dramatic performance results. Once you're in good shape, further results are more subtle and are harder to achieve.

After three years of insane productivity, our rapid growth began to slow. We were profitable and still doing well, but from 2005 to 2007, we reported only 12 percent to 15 percent annualized growth. I came to understand later that holes in our infrastructure were keeping us from breaking out—really a topic for the last stages of a start-up—but at the time it felt like the seven-year itch in a relationship: Things were going OK, but I missed the excitement of the hunt and I had gotten a little too smug and comfortable. And bored. During those more languid years, two of my best employees decided to leave and pursue other opportunities. We'll call these two women Meghan and Deanna.

Meghan was a superstar who worked hard, was highly intelligent, and was dedicated to success. In short, she was pretty much everything you would want an employee to be. This was her first job out of college, and she had been knocking her assignments out of the park with fantastic production for eighteen consecutive months. She was one of six full-time employees at this time, and we were in the process of hiring new people she would train. Then the company's growth began to slow, and her stellar returns started coming back down to earth. Months earlier we had laid out some specific and incentive-laden opportunities for advancement for her, but with the company's once frenzied growth slowing down, the timeline we had established was being extended. When her lightning-fast career trajectory slowed, Meghan seemed to lose her mojo. Like any rookie who experiences immediate success, the inevitable setbacks carry more weight than they would for a more seasoned pro. She experienced the dreaded sophomore slump.

But Meghan was a results-driven person. She found a new job with one of our competitors in another city. Ouch. It's tempting to feel angry or vindictive when someone's decision negatively affects your company. My first reaction was to feel betrayed. I'm glad I didn't blurt out what I was really thinking when she handed me her letter. We talked. I thought about things. I better understood why she needed to go. She was searching for a fresh start in a new town. Maybe the same thing I would have done in her place.

She left with grace and professionalism. In our exit interview, I expressed my sincere disappointment that she was leaving. I made sure Meghan knew what an asset she had been. I liked and trusted her and felt my company benefited from her presence. After she left, our bottom line suffered as I had expected—in the short term. Production went down. Morale swooned too, as Meghan's two-person department lost half its manpower. Not insurmountable damage, but damage nonetheless.

As if losing a great rainmaker while enduring slowing company growth wasn't enough of a challenge, we lost Deanna, our office manager, during the same period. She had been with the company for several years. This turned out to be a simple case of not knowing what you have until it's gone. That's my gentle way of admitting that we—I—took her for granted. When we hired Deanna, she performed an administrative role at a company with $1 million in revenue. But as our business grew, her role expanded into something more closely resembling true office and facilities management in a company three times its original size. Consequently, Deanna had to manage three times the responsibility and three times the headaches, and keep three times as many people happy, all for virtually the same salary she received when she began. And with no help. Oops.

At the time, I had no idea what the market was for office managers, and I thought her salary was appropriate for the position. I wasn't cheap; I was just ignorant, which became abundantly clear when she accepted a similar position making substantially more than what we had been paying her. I felt like a miserly jerk for underpaying her so significantly, but I was pretty certain we couldn't put a counteroffer on her new salary, especially with our slowing growth. Or so I thought. Sure, I was sorry to see Deanna go, but I was excited to see someone I cared about make such a huge career leap. I knew we could take care of things just fine. *Uh-oh.* It wasn't until she was gone that I realized all the ways that Deanna was worth every penny the other company was paying, and I should have countered their offer with a raise.

While I looked for a replacement for Deanna, one of my friends came in to serve as a short-term bandage for the empty position. She agreed to keep us alive by sending invoices, maintaining payroll, and ensuring the lights stayed on, but we all knew this was a temporary fix.

Our first new office manager came from a staffing agency. She lasted a grand total of three days. The skills on her resume were hardly reflected on the job. She ruined many of the projects she worked on and created more work for me. I figured it was just bad luck and hired another replacement through another agency.

Unlike "Ms. Three Days on the Job," our second office manager was capable, intelligent, and immensely likeable. But her passion for the job and our company just didn't seem to be there. Office management is regimented, highly specific, repetitive work that requires unwavering attention to detail. Our new employee thought she wanted to run an office, but she seemed to struggle with every task. Her job was to manage the office so I could focus on external issues like clients and candidates. We all really liked her, but it was obvious she belonged in a more creative, flexible position. All of a sudden, payroll was getting messed up, reports were incorrect, and the office atmosphere was generally deteriorating. I repeatedly had to correct her work, which took me away from my role as CEO. In short, this was hurting the company. If I was focusing on payroll, I wasn't leveraging my strengths as a leader to help my firm grow.

Notice the differences between these two personnel losses. Although there were temporary revenue reductions when Meghan left, the pain we experienced was nothing compared to trying to replace Deanna. Her operational role was essential for our company to run smoothly. It became increasingly clear that wasn't happening without her.

The one bright spot amid all this upheaval was that the company began to grow in new ways as a result of Meghan and Deanna's departures. In their exit interviews, they were very forthcoming about things we could do better—things we *had* to do better. We took careful notes and began implementing them. Just as importantly, we kept the option of their returning wide open. You can't always do that, but there was a mutual sense that perhaps this chapter of working together was not closed. Because we kept the door open for the future when they left, both Meghan and Deanna had a genuine interest in giving feedback that might improve the company. We were able to integrate their constructive criticism into our existing plans and processes to create a stronger infrastructure.

Keeping the Conversation Alive

When Meghan and Deanna left, they both expressed a concern about the opportunities for advancement and long-term careers within the company. We addressed these concerns after they left by creating written job descriptions and documented paths for promotion. We also began measuring quality in new ways and raising the level of professionalism. We missed our former employees, but we were also evolving from a bold little lifestyle business into a platform company with a defined purpose and direction, thanks in large measure to their feedback.

 There is something that is much more scarce, something rarer than ability. It is the ability to recognize ability.
—Robert Half

All the while, we kept in touch with Meghan and Deanna. I talked to both of them periodically, and so did others in the company. This is a testament to how important they were to the group; rather than disappearing from our collective memory, Meghan and Deanna both remained at the top of our consciousness. They had been great to work with, and they left with professionalism, so there was no reason not to stay in touch. And I had left the door open, hoping that they might return. Surprisingly, they came back to us at the same time. Like getting back together with an ex, there was a courtship period where we all tried to determine what had changed and whether rekindling the relationship was a good idea. The more people we interviewed for the office manager position, the more we realized Deanna was still the best fit. Deanna didn't want to be an administrator forever, and we were happy to create a different path for her advancement. The office manager role had grown as quickly as the company, so we made it a priority to figure out how to increase the salary and responsibilities. Meanwhile, Meghan returned to us looking for a new job. Her desire to try new things had given way to a strong desire to find a niche where she could fully dedicate herself. She tried out several roles in our company until settling into one that fit both her skills and interests and our needs.

By not burning bridges when two great employees took the opportunity to leave and see what else was out there, we gained insight into what we needed for our own growth and they both came back ready to make major contributions to the future of the company. Meghan and Deanna had been free to explore, and they realized they were happier with us. Because there had been no harsh words, it was easy for them to come back. We took their parting advice to heart and acted on it. In the end, they returned to our new, more grown-up company, and with them the business really took off. They brought knowledge and dedication that helped solidify our new direction.

Keep Your Great Employees Close— Even When They're Gone

Hire people, not positions. Hire people for life—even if they don't reciprocate the feeling at the time. Create a compelling environment where your employees can reach their individual goals. It doesn't mean they'll stick around when things get tough and crazy in start-up mode, but it improves the chances that they will. Remember, if you choose good people and they give you good information and feedback, they will improve your company— even if they move on.

When employees leave, encourage them to talk about the reasons why and create an atmosphere that welcomes honest feedback about how to build and improve your business. If you've got a hothead who just wants to put you in your place, let him or her have at it. There might still be one valuable lesson you can gain. When I first started out, I had trouble keeping my ego in check and didn't want to hear criticism about my company—or me. But that has become much easier over the years. And I've learned that when you listen to people as they leave and make appropriate changes, sometimes the great employees will come back.

Breaking Up With Class

Do	Don't
• Express sincere disappointment.	• Lay on the guilt trip.
• Set up a time to talk more thoroughly after the initial emotional shock has worn off.	• Make any rash promises or threats.
• Look at things from the other person's perspective.	• Take a resignation as an attack on you as a manager or your overall company concept.
• Get feedback from others on whether there was something that could have been done better to retain this talented person.	• Criticize this person to others and question things like his or her loyalty or overall value to the company.
• Give the person who is leaving plenty of space to express his or her true feelings about the strengths and weaknesses of your company.	• Explain to the person how he or she is making a mistake or not under-standing how good this person has it working with you.

If you have employees you value highly, give them your blessing to do what they feel they must do, and leave open the option to come back—or create new ways to work together as vendors or customers or in joint partnerships. Who knows? Maybe they can keep making cash for you. It may be tempting to lock doors, burn bridges, and emotionally move on once they've left, but no doubt you know how hard it is to find employees who truly fit a company's mission and culture. If you put a bolt on the door and make it clear that their leaving is a permanent decision, you will, at a minimum, miss out on valuable insight into your company. Rather than wishing for great new employees, consider keeping in touch with the ones who have left. Seeing the realities of life and business at other companies might make it easier for them to appreciate your good company and return to you dedicated for the long haul.

King Lear was one of Shakespeare's great tragedies—both the play and the man. In fact, this is a bedtime story that can put you to sleep earlier than you want—though it is filled with some great lessons. When Lear tested his three daughters to see who loved him most—a bad idea from the start—his two schemers, who, along with their husbands, lusted after his throne. They were quick with flattery and showy gifts. His third daughter, Cordelia, refused to play the game and simply pointed to the quality of her life with him as all the proof of her love that he needed. With his ego bruised over her lack of flowery words and special gifts for him, he banished her from his presence, though Cordelia was the one who was truly loyal and most loved him. In breaking this cord of love, he brought ruin on himself and his family.

Losing an employee or customer isn't nearly as dramatic as a Shakespearean tragedy—though if it comes at the wrong time, it sure can feel like it. Burning bridges because of anger or a wounded ego still has the potential to do serious damage to your enterprise.

The Moral of the Story

Anticipate inevitable turnover in the ups and downs of starting a new company. Minimize the negative impact by maintaining and affirming relationships with your best employees—even if they leave. Learn lessons every time someone leaves.

For Reflection and Action

1. When someone quits, do you take it as an insult or sign of disloyalty? Do you take things personally—and express things personally? Have you ever hired anyone back?

2. Do you conduct exit interviews? Do you listen to and truly implement constructive ideas that you receive from people who leave your company?

3. Have you ever called a former employee a year after his or her departure and asked what you could do differently that would make the person consider returning to your company?

4. Is there someone who has formerly worked for you whom you should at least reach out to right now?

Chapter 4

DON'T ISOLATE YOURSELF

Here is the basic rule for winning success. Let's mark it in
the mind and remember it. The rule is: Success depends on
the support of other people. The only hurdle between you
and what you want to be in is the support of other people.

—David J. Schwartz

A FEW YEARS AGO, I WAS invited to attend a meeting of
the Virginia Council of CEOs at Richmond's famed
Jefferson Hotel, complete with an elegant lunch and a
message from an informative, compelling speaker. While I'm
sure the event focused on a relevant topic and presentation,
what I remember most about my first exposure to this impressive group was that at my table everyone was smiling. All of them.
They were friendly and unhurried, and seemed like they really
wanted to be there. They weren't just cramming in another lunch
meeting while preoccupied with afternoon appointments.

This group has very specific criteria for applying, becoming a
member, and maintaining membership. The three requirements
for membership are:

- You must be the one person ultimately in charge of
  profit and loss.
- Your company must meet minimum revenue
  requirements.
- Your company must be in an expansion mode.

This group doesn't give or solicit advice during their meetings; they meet only to share experiences, following the model in Mo Fathelbab's book *FORUM: The Secret Advantage of Successful Leaders.*

Based on several positive meetings that I had attended as a guest, I decided to complete the application process. While I had already had my advisory board in place for several years at this point, I still felt like something was missing from my path of growth as a CEO, business owner, and individual. As an entrepreneur, I had to encourage my own personal development, and provide my own continuing education program. I also felt like this group would help me become more aware of and involved in the local business community. I had no idea that many of the people I would often see socially ran their own businesses. And after getting a taste of this particular group, I decided that I needed a separate place to work *on* my business, not *in* my business. This felt like the right forum.

My Night at the Round Table

I was right. After attending several speaker events, I was placed in a small discussion group called a roundtable. This was where the magic happened. The group usually consisted of about ten CEOs from various industries who were carefully selected by an executive committee to avoid any conflicts of interest. The most important component of the roundtable was the presence of trust, established with an absolute commitment to confidentiality. Not even spouses are privy to information shared in conversations around the table. Sure, we might make jokes along the lines of, "What happens in Vegas stays in Vegas," but we took this privacy seriously. What we shared in these roundtables absolutely stayed in that room. Ironically, this strict rule created a real freedom of expression I have yet to see anywhere else. It's hard to explain just how valuable the exchange of ideas really was—unless you've participated in this kind of group setting.

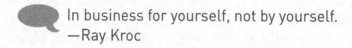

In business for yourself, not by yourself.
—Ray Kroc

Membership in this group is no small time commitment; members must attend a four-hour meeting each month, no excuses, and we all know that four hours on a workday multiplies like dog years. And—if you can believe this—no cell phones or e-mail is allowed during the time together. CEOs without BlackBerrys or iPhones! These gatherings truly provide an intense time of growth and introspection.

I'll never forget the first roundtable meeting I attended. It was held at The Crossings, a resort just northwest of Richmond, on a hot day in August. While I typically view myself as a gregarious, fun-loving guy, some people would be surprised to know that Myers-Briggs* classifies me as an introvert. Interaction in a group setting doesn't energize me, it saps my energy. I don't relish opening up in a personal way to strangers. I don't know if I was particularly nervous that day because it was my first small-group meeting, or if the resort turned the air conditioning to economy mode, but I remember distinctly how it felt to sit around a sterile boardroom table with a group of perfect strangers and sweat my way through the getting-to-know-you part.

The meeting was facilitated by Mo Fathelbab, using his well-defined process that allows members in a peer group to learn by sharing experiences, not through the quid pro quo process of

---

* The Myers-Briggs Type Indicator (MBTI) assessment is a psychometric questionnaire designed to measure psychological preferences in how people perceive the world and make decisions.

giving and receiving advice. Part of the breaking-the-ice process involves using a tool Mo calls a "lifeline."

The exercise basically called for us to convey our life stories in a way that illustrated the significance of events and emotional impact they had on our lives. I remember sharing the high points of getting married, the births of my children, starting my own business, watching my boys catch their first fish without my help, and other positives that were not much different from others I heard that day.

But what I remember most clearly from the lifeline exercise were the low points. The battle my mom fought and eventually lost with cancer, determining that I did not have the physical ability to become a professional athlete and needed to get a real job, writing a check out of my HELOC to make payroll, personally experiencing the "Peter Principle" at a previous employer where everyone truly did rise to the level of his or her incompetence. I've come across this lifeline worksheet a few times since then. It's not something I'll ever throw away, because it really does put things in perspective. Life is a mixed bag of good and bad, no matter how you shake it. Or as Forrest Gump's mom would say, "Life's a box of chocolates, Forrest. You never know what you're gonna get" (*Forrest Gump*, 1994).

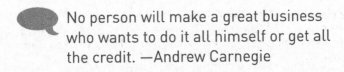 No person will make a great business who wants to do it all himself or get all the credit. —Andrew Carnegie

Most important to my business life was the liberating experience of being in a room with a group of peers who faced some of the same challenges I had. It was downright invigorating to share the good, the bad, and the ugly with a group of people whose primary responsibility right then was just to listen. And while I don't remember everyone's stories, I immediately felt like I knew these people inside and out. I wasn't stranded alone on a deserted island anymore. In this group I had found an oasis—a place to rest my parched and weary soul. I'm still grateful for them.

In chapter 2, I wrote about the importance of an advisory board. This discussion group is not an advisory board, but a group of people that are facing the same challenges that I am, both professionally and personally. We do not focus only on the economy, politics, and business strategies. In fact, while I haven't kept track of the topics that we've covered, I bet they are half personal and half business. Before my involvement with this group, I sometimes felt as though it was just me against the world while running my business. I discovered that there are many other people out there building businesses. The ability to speak freely with them about the real pressures that I face has been exhilarating.

I am not sure how I made it without advisors and peers who were in the trenches with me. I did realize the need for two distinct types of feedback and interaction. I needed a group to maintain an absolutely objective perspective on my leadership and my business, and I needed a group for emotional encouragement and to help me grow as a person.

Everyone Needs a Support Network

My deserted island analogy is perhaps dramatic, but that doesn't mean it isn't true. It perfectly illustrates what a saving grace a group of peers can be to a business owner. Entrepreneurs are often captains of their own ships. If there's a shipwreck, mutiny, or rough seas ahead, we can easily feel like we've ended up marooned on a desert island. This isolation might often hit you in the middle of the night when everyone else in the house is sound asleep. Even if you sleep solo, you know as well as I do that middle-of-the-night quiet is anything but peaceful. This is when a multitude of scenarios dance in and out of your consciousness. Your head rings with multiple voices of what-ifs and, *What should I do about XYZ?*

 Don't walk in front of me, I may not follow. Don't walk behind me, I may not lead. Walk beside me, and just be my friend. —Albert Camus

That's why it's incredibly gratifying, and more so necessary, to surround yourself with people who understand your experiences, even if they just nod and say, "Yup, been there, done that, and lived to tell." Through these gatherings, I've learned that the problems I face are not essentially different from anyone else's, even if particular circumstances and factors are highly varied.

Peer groups like the one I found—or the one that found me, depending upon your view of fate and karma—are an invaluable resource. Entrepreneurs and CEOs need a safe haven where they can let it all hang out without worrying that their challenges will be viewed as a sign of vulnerability or defeat to potential customers or employees. When you spend every day and many sleepless nights figuring out how to maintain and further your company's livelihood, it's incredibly helpful and reenergizing to step away from that heady responsibility and network with professional peers who are outside your chain of command.

Two things make my group serve that reenergizing purpose for me. Number one: It's not the place to go for business advice. In fact, "no advice" is one of the rules. Rather, it's simply a safe place to unload our frustrations as well as our joys and provide support to others who are chewing on the same dirt on the way to achieving the American dream. In any given meeting, you might hear the CEO sitting next to you chime in that she's gone through something similar and explain how she handled it, or you may just find comfort in the fact that ten people are listening to you without any sort of what's-in-it-for-me agenda or judgment. You can ask questions like: *How did you solve this particular cash flow issue in your own business? How did you deal with a difficult customer who was a significant portion of your business? How did you deal with a personal family tragedy while still being responsible for running your own business?* You won't receive direct advice, but you will gain insight from another's experience. And when we share our burdens this way, it makes the load seem lighter.

The second thing that makes the group work is our commonality as entrepreneurs and business owners. Sure, there are many capable coaches, consultants, and experts in the marketplace, but a group of people who, like you, run their own businesses—with their own mortgages, family livelihoods, and reputations on the line—share your perspective in a unique way. And, truth be told, when there are ten entrepreneurs sitting around the table, there are very few issues that someone in the room has not faced in one way or another.

Consider this classic bedtime story that is still relevant today: Alexander Selkirk grew up in a prosperous family and enjoyed success of his own at a young age as an English privateer—a polite way of saying he was a government-sanctioned pirate. But on one sea journey, he had such bitter conflict with the captain of his ship that he demanded to be put ashore on a deserted island. He volunteered to be marooned. When he was found four years later, he was a physical marvel but had lost much of his vocabulary and ability to socialize. He gained more wealth on the way back to Scotland and added to that by telling the story of his survival, which became a popular pamphlet in the early eighteenth century. His story, in fact, was the inspiration for Daniel Defoe's classic character, Robinson Crusoe.

Selkirk was never able to fit into civilization again. Despite a beautiful home with servants, he chose to live alone in a cave on his property. None of us are ever going to volunteer to be marooned or let ourselves become that isolated—though on some days the life of a start-up entrepreneurial feels that way. Like Robinson Crusoe on his deserted island, we all need to find a "Friday" to connect with, someone who will listen without judgment, someone who is in the same boat—or island—as we are.

Networking as an Entrepreneur

Yes, you will attend many functions and meet many people for the purpose of expanding your influence and finding new customers. But don't forget your need for simple, affirming, no-agenda friendship. Here are a few ideas to consider:

1. Chamber of commerce—It is assumed that men and women who attend chamber or Rotary or similar organizational meetings are there to hand out business cards. But there are also many events planned just for getting to know others in similar fields.

2. Back to school—Check out your local university to see if there are select courses you would like to take or audit on an occasional basis. Get tuned in to the business program's calendar. Many schools bring in guest speakers and create other stimulating opportunities for students and local business leaders.

3. Keep the faith—Do you regularly attend church or synagogue or another faith setting? An entire microcosm of the population will be present, including many other business owners. Ask your pastor if there is a special meeting time for businesspeople to find fellowship.

4. Social networking—LinkedIn, Facebook, Twitter, small business and entrepreneurial forums: all of these online points of connection have ways for you to search for, connect to, and interact with people in similar positions as you. Can this take the place of face-to-face interaction? I don't think so, but there is a reason these services have exploded.

5. Blogging—Use programs like digg.com to track the blogs of other entrepreneurs. Like social networking, this can't take the place of face-to-face interaction, but it still keeps you in touch with what others are experiencing. I hope you'll stop by and visit me and catch some of my fresh reflections on entrepreneurialism at www.15bedtimestories.com.

6. Be a self-starter—Contact a few friends and associates and start your own weekly or monthly meeting to talk through challenges and successes of being an entrepreneur.

The Moral of the Story

In addition to business advisors, you need a support system of people who are facing similar issues and challenges as you. No matter what form it takes, it is essential to act now to incorporate others into your life to be successful.

For Reflection and Action

1. Where do you turn for peer support?

2. Are you part of a group of people—or do you meet regularly with even one person—who have been through what you've been through, who face similar challenges, with whom you feel comfortable speaking?

3. Do you have a place where you can work on yourself—the CEO—as a person, and not just improve your business skills? In other words, do you have a truly safe environment where you can "let it all hang out"?

4. Take a few minutes right now to jot down the outline of a plan that will help you experience recurring opportunities to relate to and connect with peers in a truly safe and confidential environment.

Chapter 5

Don't Compromise Your Ethics

If you don't have integrity, you have nothing. You can't buy it. You can have all the money in the world, but if you are not a moral and ethical person, you really have nothing.

—Henry Kravis

ONE BAD APPLE SPOILS THE barrel. Guess what? It only takes one unethical company to spoil the playing field for everyone else. And it only takes one unethical decision to put a question mark next to your reputation forever.

No matter your industry, invariably there are certain stereotypes you must overcome. Lawyers? *Egotistical and overpaid.* Car salesmen? *Fast-talking swindlers.* Accountants? *Stiff, dry, boring, and a little too creative with numbers.* You get the picture. Now, obviously, for most professionals, these stereotypes are a far cry from the truth. Unfortunately, the few folks living up to these assumptions ruin the image for the rest of us.

My field, the executive search business, is no different from any other business where there are people who seem to stray from what is clearly recognized to be ethically correct behavior. Most corporations view headhunters as a necessary evil. There are plenty of bad apples in my world who are motivated by short-term dollars rather than long-term relationships. Some companies in my industry treat placements solely as a commodity or a quota to fill. They overlook the value of long-term client relationships and play their placements like a game of chess, moving these pawns from corporation to corporation, all in the name of quick results—and profits. To them, above-board ethical reasoning means nothing when pockets are open under the table.

Fall of the House of Enron

No other name is more synonymous with business fraud than that of Ken Lay, founder and CEO of Enron, once the world's seventh-largest company, which collapsed spectacularly in 2001. The son of a minister, he vigorously defended himself until his death in 2006, while awaiting final sentencing—expected to be life in prison. Few others defended the man who led a company found guilty of countless trade and finance infractions. More than $60 billion in market value disappeared overnight, along with thousands of jobs and the legacy of a man who seemingly lived the American dream.

Those guys give us a bad name. But in reality, most recruiters—the ethical ones—are focused on building long-term relationships with their clients and on ensuring that their clients' business objectives are met. Since most companies can't afford sophisticated internal recruiting departments, they often outsource placement to an agency that can fill their needs. When guided by integrity, genuine service firms allow their clients to focus on their core business rather than the distraction caused by the turmoil of turnover, which is compounded when the service company approaches the very same person with a new offer.

A Few Bad Apples I Know

When I started my business, we performed only executive search services. The nature of this niche has a way of guarding against unethical behavior because the technical expertise and track record of success required means competition is limited. To be honest, we didn't have the temptation to put placements in a revolving door like some competitors did. Once we switched to more general placement services, however, I started realizing our new, larger playing field opened up confrontations with my value system on several fronts. Here I was, the owner of a business that honestly subscribed to the American Staffing Association's Code of Ethics when conducting every one of our placements, and suddenly, I was getting calls from clients who were worried we would steal their employees and add them to a roster of have-gun-will-travel mercenaries, just as other search firms were doing to them.

I was shocked by these concerns and disappointed in my competitors. Because of someone else's unethical conduct, we were guilty by association. From day one, I have believed and adhered to the industry rule that you do not recruit from your clients. Period. The relationship between your company and a client is built on honest and genuine intentions. But we need contracts for a reason. It wasn't enough that industry standards and codes dictated that you shouldn't recruit from someone who is paying you money to find new employees. Because of bad apples in the industry who break that rule consistently, this stipulation had to be added to our contracts.

As a business owner, I would not intend to cause any harm to a company that I depend on for success. Now, to the outsider, this sounds like a fairly obvious conclusion. But then I started seeing the bad apples in action.

While at a prospective placement one day, I walked in with our candidate and saw someone I recognized interviewing for another position. When a representative from this person's search firm arrived, I realized that we had competed on a deal two weeks prior. We had lost. This isn't just sour grapes on my part. The consultant he'd placed and been paid for in that deal was the same person at this interview—interviewing for another position! Even though there was a commitment to one client, the search firm was fishing around at other accounts using the same bait. I was livid.

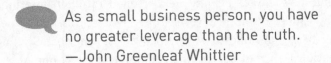

> As a small business person, you have no greater leverage than the truth.
> —John Greenleaf Whittier

Each time I saw this type of unethical behavior, it became harder and harder for me to sleep at night. Through the grapevine of disgruntled customers and industry professionals, I started hearing stories about other firms recruiting employees from clients, placing them elsewhere, and then calling the former employer to have them rehired. Or they'd place an individual in one company, pull him out for another placement, and then put him back with the original employer—and get paid for both gigs. We even found one of our competitors making changes to an e-mail time-and-date stamp to make it look like they worked with and submitted a candidate before we did. It seemed that at every opportunity, my competitors were taking advantage of the integrity I worked so hard to uphold.

Sadly, over the years, I've realized this type of behavior just happens. The bad apples keep spoiling the barrel, making even the good ones appear rotten.

In order to disassociate my company from the rancid bunch, I realized the importance of maintaining an uncompromising ethical stance and promoting that as a key component of my company's brand within the marketplace. Every day we reinforce why we're different, and we try to change the industry by talking about our ethics, values, and long-standing, relationship-based success stories. We put in our contracts that we will not solicit a client's current employees without their giving us express permission to do so. We also do not bad-mouth our competitors when competing for placements. No matter how poorly we might think of the values and motivations guiding a competitor's decisions and actions, we won't play that game. And our clients always respond positively. Eight years later, I'm still in business and growing. Some of the worst offenders of our industry's code of conduct are prospering too. But some have fallen by the wayside. And I haven't seen any of the cheaters outperform us over time.

Ultimately, building and promoting a positive image in a marketplace that has its share of questionable ethics has helped me sleep better at night. At the end of the day, I can look in the mirror and know that we are not headed toward the slippery slope that unprincipled greed can create. Once you've chosen that path, backing up is nearly impossible. It's called a slippery slope for a reason.

In the end, short-term gains are never worth allowing unethical decisions to spoil the business you've worked so hard to grow.

Take the High Road

You will find lasting success when you operate with integrity and adhere to a set of honorable ethics—and you'll sleep better at night too. You must run your business with the same morals and ethics that drive your day-to-day life. The owner and the business are one; consequently, you can't distinguish between business values and your values. Especially in the early stages of your startup, it is important to create and incorporate a set of values and practices that everyone in your organization not only follows but also believes in. That set of morals and ethics can serve as a rudder during difficult times.

 The superior man understands what is right; the inferior man understands what will sell. —Confucius

You can be successful on the high road, even if it seems the competition is making gains by taking the low road. Once a few clients get burned by the so-called competition, those gains will go up in smoke as word spreads throughout the industry. But don't focus on your competition's questionable practices; instead, highlight the positive ethics and integrity that set you apart. Doing so will open up great opportunities for you, because long-term achievement is built on satisfied, loyal clients.

Inevitably, employees and the company reflect the personality of the CEO. I have found that when I strive to maintain my ethical business identity, brand, and relationships, my people take pride in the fact that we actually do operate differently from some of our competitors.

For the start-up entrepreneur, here are five keys to building an ethical company:

1. Establish an open environment where employees can voice concerns, including issues with company policy, without fear of recrimination. We see examples every day where people blow the whistle—think Enron—and the authorities must step in. It should never come to that.

2. Clearly communicate what ethical conduct must look like in your company. Don't assume everyone knows what is right and wrong. And don't assume they *know* what it is. As your company grows, these expectations will need to become more formalized.

3. Deal decisively and immediately with breaches in conduct. Make sure you get the whole story, particularly looking for ways the company might have pressured someone to act unethically. But be ready to respond in a way that is appropriate for and fits the act.

4. You and your leaders must be examples. Ethical behavior must start at the top if it is to be pervasive in your company.

5. Make sure you reward people on the basis of exhibiting company values. Often, but not always, this is tied to performance factors.

In Alexandre Dumas' classic novel, *The Count of Monte Cristo,* three jealous friends conspire to send Edmond Dantes to a life sentence in the dreaded island prison, Chateau d'If. Dantes loses his career, his family, and his Mercedes—no mere automobile, she was the love of his life. But in this enduring tale of revenge and mercy, it is obvious that those who defrauded Dantes lost so much more, even before experiencing revenge at the hand of the Count of Monte Cristo.

Your story as a captain of enterprise may never become one of the bestselling books of all time or make it to the silver screen, but a clean conscience is its own reward.

The Moral of the Story

Acting unethically may lead to some immediate business benefits and successes, but in the long term, the dynamics of a successful company—good reputation, strong relationships, loyalty, and customer trust—derive from strong values and high levels of ethical conduct. In your personal life as well, integrity will always outweigh unethical gains.

For Reflection and Action

1. In your field of business, what are the main pressures to act unethically? Is unethical conduct pervasive?

2. How do integrity and ethics play out in your company? Consider financial and relational aspects, as well as any areas that are specific to your industry. Does your company adhere to a written code of ethics?

3. How do you maintain a companywide commitment to the code? Is every employee aware of that commitment? Have they signed an agreement to uphold company ethics?

4. When you're making a pitch for business, do you compare your company to the competition? Do you do so by bad-mouthing them?

5. Can you think of a situation during your career in which you didn't perform ethically? How do you view that outcome now? What should you have done differently?

Chapter 6

DON'T AVOID CONFRONTATION

When you confront a problem you begin to solve it.
—Rudy Giuliani

L AST SUMMER I WAS SITTING in the bleachers watching my boys play baseball. I usually coach them, but that season I had decided to take a break and just be a spectator. This was their first year of kid pitch, and I knew I was in for a long, but fulfilling, day. It was cold, and there were only a few people in the bleachers. My wife and daughter had opted for grocery shopping, so I was there by myself. Wimps.

Next to me sat another dad enjoying the game. Around the third inning, the game started to drag on, and Robert and I struck up a conversation. I didn't know him very well, but learned he had his own business, a consulting firm that focused on supply chain issues in the textile industry. We immediately started talking shop, probably a no-no for a youth baseball game, but something a lot of us entrepreneurs can't keep ourselves from doing. By the second inning, we were deep into the challenges of owning one's own company. Robert shared a personal story that piqued my attention because it was relevant to a situation I had recently gotten into: a customer that bullies you and your team because they know how important they are to you.

His company opened in 2001 during a crippling time in the country's economy. The Internet bubble had just popped. Professionals were losing their jobs. Fortunes were lost on business models made out of air and hype and little substance. Retirement accounts evaporated as WorldCom, Enron, and other companies imploded. And there he was in the middle of it— investing his life's savings in a start-up while every newspaper page he turned seemed to tell him to do otherwise. But believing his plan had potential, he was determined to make this business succeed. Robert was my kind of guy!

He had landed a pretty good-sized firm in the first several months of opening his business. He was thrilled to sign up a substantial textile company, even if he offered them a deep discount in order to secure the account. They were, after all, sending him a lot of projects. This would keep the lights turned on while he found customers that would pay the full industry rate for his services. That's why he got particularly excited about his second customer. It was a start-up carpet company in Charlotte, North Carolina, which needed to add some overseas suppliers. The company was a referral from a former associate and good friend of his who believed that the company was going to really take off, becoming a real cash cow.

Robert gave me the broad brushstrokes of his arrangement with this new client. Even though the rate was right, the deal wasn't perfect because it included a less-than-ideal payment plan—net forty-five days in an industry that is net ten days. He said that this should have set off some warning bells in the back of his mind. After all, he was putting a lot on the line, especially as a young company with serious cash flow challenges of its own. But in his inexperience—and maybe a little sense of desperation—he felt that he needed to be more flexible. He got right to work for this company and was able to set them up with some new cost-saving suppliers and distribution systems within a couple weeks. His contacts there were very pleased with his work. But when the account payable date hit, he got a call from their purchasing department and was told they needed an extra forty-five days to pay. He only had two clients at the time—and one was heavily discounted—so he found it difficult to cut them off without giving them opportunity to follow up on their promise. After all, they were a start-up, too. So he still wasn't ready to stand his ground and insist that they uphold the already generous payment terms. He felt as though he had no choice but to agree to an extension. He agreed to the deal, but insisted he needed the money for all services provided in full on day ninety and no later.

Up to this point, he had been dealing with the finance director of the company, but because of the size of the late payment and his insistence on full pay at ninety days, this director connected him with the CEO. The CEO told Robert that they were looking to raise more capital, but regardless, the company would have the money to pay him in full at ninety days. He was warm, apologetic, and charming. Robert's fears were allayed.

Fast-forward a few weeks. The deadline quickly approached. My bleacher-mate needed his money. He was perpetuating the slow-pay cycle with some of his vendors. When you have only two clients, forty-five days is a long time to go without payment, but ninety days, well, that begins to feel like a search for water in the Sahara after your jug has just run dry.

Obviously, he was becoming anxious. When he touched base with his contact, he affirmed how happy he was with the systems provided—and that they had several new projects they wanted him to tackle—so he knew the first round of payment delays wasn't based on performance. He called a few days ahead of the deadline to verify that everything was on track.

He tried the director of finance and got no call back. He tried the CEO. Same result. He called their purchasing agent whom he had helped put new supply protocols in place. No answer. He called every person in the company whom he had met, including the receptionist. No one returned his calls. Uh oh.

Ninety days came and went. He felt betrayed. Angry. Bitter. Most of all, worried.

Robert was forty years old at the time, had invested a substantial amount of his own money in this small specialty business, and now his family's savings were on the line. He was questioning his decision to follow a dream of being his own boss. Had he made a bad decision that would put his family in bankruptcy?

What to Do When You're Not Invincible

Until this moment, Robert said that his emotions had been mitigated by a sense of invincibility. Everything always works out in the end. Again, I could relate. I had been there. Many entrepreneurs develop an incredible feeling of empowerment when starting a new enterprise. He kept ignoring the warning alarms on this deal because he had been inspired by the freedom of taking business decisions into his own hands. Personal ownership of a company and doing something he believed in had energized him from day one. He was relieved to no longer feel his fate was controlled by the powers above him. No one was going to tap him on the shoulder and tell him that they wanted to see him in the conference room so he could be told he didn't have a job anymore.

But with his start-up company's future now looking questionable, Robert's sense of invincibility was shaken. To the core. Robert's fears had been realized. Ninety days had come and gone with no check. He had trusted this company—more specifically, he had trusted a fellow CEO who seemed like an honorable guy—to keep his word and honor his contract. The client had used his services and profited from them, only to shut him out. Robert told me that his inclination was to move on and consider this a tough lesson learned; he was not comfortable with confrontations. But his financial situation didn't allow that luxury. He realized it was now up to him to make something happen.

Since his client wouldn't communicate with him, he decided to fly to Charlotte for a face-to-face confrontation. And while the CEO didn't know Robert was coming, my friend made sure to verify that he would be in the office that day. He was going to set up camp in the lobby and stay until he had a direct conversation with the CEO. His goal? Return home with money in hand. He booked his flight and arrived at the airport, refusing to acknowledge how nervous he felt at the impending confrontation.

I was just shaking my head at this point in the story. I wondered if I would have done the same thing. Maybe I would have thought a last-minute airfare was a waste of money, maybe not.

Upon arrival, Robert jumped in his rental car and headed to the client's office. When he announced to the receptionist that he was there to see the CEO, she reported that the CEO would be in meetings all day. He responded, "No problem. Let him know I'll wait." The CEO came out to greet him in the lobby an hour later. The CEO was all smiles, but the message was clear: *You're not coming near my office because this is going to be a quick meeting.* After some small talk about how great the weather was, my friend got down to business.

"You made a promise to pay your invoice in full. Not only are you not doing that, you won't even return my calls. You are not honoring your contract or your word."

The CEO was no longer smiling. He didn't want the receptionist to hear anymore so he took Robert by the shoulder and sheepishly told him that business was good but cash flow was still a problem. He assured him not to worry because they were making progress in raising another round of funding to get them over the valley they were in right now.

Robert actually felt some pangs of sympathy right then. After all, the client was struggling in start-up mode, too. Robert also didn't feel good about the fact that he had showed up unannounced to collect the money. It seemed a little over-the-top at the moment. He even felt a flash of guilt. But he thought of his own bank account and unpaid vendors, mustered his courage, and stayed on task. No, he didn't collect the check then, but he did let the CEO know: No more excuses, no more taking advantage of my lenience. The CEO profusely apologized for the delay and said the funds would be at Robert's bank by wire the next

Thursday. They shook hands and looked each other in the eye. Robert flew back home, at ease in his mind that the money would be coming and that he would be able to stay in business.

The next Thursday came and went. No money. He called the CEO to find out what was going on, but there was no response. Same thing with the finance director and others on his list. To say he was frustrated was an understatement.

No More Denial

The CEO had looked him in the eye, shaken his hand, and given his personal assurance that he would be paid. That had to count for something, right? The answer was obvious. No more denial. The client was taking advantage of him. After this three-month wild goose chase for money, he knew he couldn't count on getting paid based on anything anyone at the company said—at least not voluntarily. For the second time he considered giving up and chalking it up to experience. But he needed the money too badly. He would have to do the same thing to some of his vendors if he let this go. So he contacted his lawyer to see what remedies were available to resolve the dilemma.

There are many reasons to have a lawyer in your corner. Access to educated, experienced, and sound advice is only one of them. His lawyer pointed out that facing a pending lawsuit would inhibit the client's ability to raise the capital needed to pay him—an implied threat that would carry some real weight. They also discussed informing overseas suppliers of the situation, but ultimately decided that would hurt his ability to connect them with new clients in the future. After much discussion, the lawyer suggested that Robert draft a "nice," mostly non-threatening letter himself, but that he end it with a specific sentence to let the CEO know that his attorney was prepared to draw up papers for a lawsuit. Robert wrote the letter that night, the attorney approved his wording immediately, and he sent it out overnight delivery with shipment tracking.

Our baseball game was winding down, but I was completely enthralled at this point in the story, desperate to know how it would end. Robert told me that he sat in front of his computer the next day watching the online tracking as the package made its way to Charlotte. Isn't technology great? Finally the status changed to "delivered." With a mix of anticipation and dread, he waited for the phone to ring.

And ring it did. Robert said that literally minutes after someone signed for the package, the CEO was in his ear. My friend was laughing as he described the call. I don't think Robert is a profane person, but he did whisper a few of the names he was called. The CEO of the company had shouted every cuss word in the English language. But aside from being amusing in retrospect, his behavior was startling. My friend had spoken to this man on numerous occasions, helping his company improve its product offering and save money, and he had always seemed professional and pleasant. And yet here he was, viciously attacking a fellow business owner for something that was his own fault.

Confrontation 101

1. Conflict is inevitable in business and in life.

2. Ignoring problems seldom makes them go away and often intensifies conflict levels.

3. If humor and indirect hints work, great. But this tactic is over-worked, usually ineffective, and a form of procrastination.

4. If you struggle to confront others, jot down an outline and a few key phrases as a script. Hit your script immediately; this is not a chit-chat kind of conversation.

5. Keep the focus on problems and issues, not personalities and relationships.

6. Make this your first call of the day, or your productivity will suffer due to preoccupation.

7. Say exactly what you want to happen to resolve the conflict. Don't call or visit until you know exactly what this is yourself.

8. Once your conflict is resolved, move on appropriately. If you can continue in a working relationship with the person you confronted, don't hold grudges.

The CEO told him they would never do business together again. Then he wired the money into his account. The urgent dismissal was a relief—though not to the degree receiving his money was. If this was how this man and his company treated people who delivered value to their company, he never wanted to work with them again anyway. Putting his company in jeopardy as they hung him out to dry over payments was not a mistake he was going to repeat.

While it's important to maintain a certain amount of flexibility with clients, especially in the initial phases of building a client base, no clothesline is worth hanging on if it's choking you. A side note to my fellow entrepreneurs who have worked in sales: As much as we love to make a sale, deep down, we all know—but need to be reminded—that not every sale is a good sale. When it's not your company, it's easy to gripe about the boss who nixed a big deal you made. When you have your own company, there will be deals you nix as well.

Trust...But Verify

You can't be afraid to be the bad guy. When you know what's right, you must take charge and do what is necessary to resolve a problem situation, regardless of what others might think about you. You might not be able to trust your instincts. If you are honest and fair, it is natural to assume that your customers and vendors will be too. Yes, listen to people's words, but don't ignore their actions. In fact, the nonverbal communication you pick up might be all they're really saying. Robert found this out the hard way.

Once a runaround begins, on money or anything else, don't be surprised if that's the direction all interactions are going to go. You have to draw the line somewhere. You have to find the balance between being accommodating and being a hard nose who is difficult to work with. If clients don't take you and your business seriously, it's likely your business will be short-lived. You have to be willing to go to the mat for your company, even if it's highly uncomfortable.

Why a whole chapter on confronting? Aren't entrepreneurs bold by nature? There are a few who are reading this book who actually need to read the message of being "flexible" more closely. You have no problems with conflict and confrontation—and might need to back off sometimes. But my experience is that even confident and articulate individuals tend to shy away from direct conflict, even to their own expense!

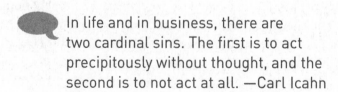 In life and in business, there are two cardinal sins. The first is to act precipitously without thought, and the second is to not act at all. —Carl Icahn

One of my favorite late-night bedtime stories is the classic Western movie *High Noon*. Sherriff Will Kane, played by Gary Cooper, marries a pacifist Quaker, played by the beautiful Grace Kelly. He turns in his badge to start a new life in a new town as a storekeeper. But then three criminal drifters show up in Hadleyville, and word gets around that a man Kane has brought to justice, Frank Miller, is on his way to this desolate little town in the New Mexico Territory, vowing revenge against Kane and anyone who helped him. The townsfolk are terrified and urge him to leave for his own safety and in hopes that Miller will forget them and pass on through. Kane decides to do that, but then in a fit of conscience, he heads back into Hadleyville to take care of unfinished business. Not dealing with Miller now will mean innocent people getting hurt, and he will always be looking over his shoulder. The people are too afraid to help—and even the deputy surrenders his badge. With his new bride threatening to leave town without him, Kane makes his stand on Main Street, one man against four.

Sometimes as a start-up CEO, it almost seems you can hear bullets whizzing past your head and feel like you're in a gunfight by yourself—at least four against one. But like Kane, you have to know that running from problems never makes them go away. Win or lose, you have to face them head-on, at high noon!

The Moral of the Story

Each of us has a personality type and a preferred way of doing business. There will come a time in any start-up when we need to take on a character role we aren't as comfortable with. This will most often be in the role of confronter.

For Reflection and Action

1. What would your first response be if you believed a client was taking advantage of your trusting nature?

2. Do you steer clear of confrontation and conflict in life—or are you comfortable with it?

3. Do you assume everyone is going to do the right thing? Or is the opposite more accurate of you; do you suspect everyone of wrongdoing until proven differently? How can both these approaches impact your business negatively?

4. Are you overly concerned about the impression you make on others?

5. Do you have legal counsel you trust?

Chapter 7

DON'T LET YOUR COMPANY DEPEND ON JUST YOU

Your ability to negotiate, communicate, influence and persuade others to do things is absolutely indispensable to everything you accomplish in life. The most effective men and women in every area are those who can quite competently organize the cooperation and assistance of other people toward the accomplishment of important goals and objectives.

—Brian Tracy

IN 2005, ONE OF MY key people asked me to sponsor a charity baseball game. His adult-league team was raising money for the Special Olympics by playing an exhibition at our local minor-league field, and he was chosen as starting pitcher. In my eyes, by sponsoring his effort, I was supporting a great cause and would also make my right-hand man happy, so I agreed. I was pleased to help out another charity, but the game was really his baby.

To be honest, after sending the check, I didn't give the event much thought—until I received a call from the emergency room. He was on the other end of the phone; somehow he had managed to shatter his arm while pitching. To hear him recount the scenario, you'd think he was playing game seven of the World Series.

It was the bottom of the inning. There was a runner on first and third. The count was one strike, two balls, two outs, and he was hoping to fool the batter with a fastball in the zone. He reared back, ready to throw a strike, and three-quarters of the way through his pitch, something went awry. The ball sailed between third and home, allowing the other team an easy score. Stunned and in pain, he looked down and saw one of his arms dangling at his side, an inch longer than the other.

"I'm done!" he yelled.

Everyone came running to see what happened. His teammates were certain it was a torn bicep or maybe even a simple sprain, but he knew they were all wrong. Thanks to a sports documentary he had watched the week before, he knew his arm was broken. The centerfielder confirmed this when he jogged over to say he'd heard the bone snap from all the way out in center field.

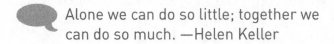

Alone we can do so little; together we can do so much. —Helen Keller

His teammates rushed him to the hospital, where doctors discovered his arm was not just broken; a bone had fractured in three pieces. To recover, he needed surgery, ten pins, a steel plate, and some real time off to recover.

My first thought when I heard about his injury was, *I hope my friend is okay*. His family had recently begun renovating their newly purchased home. I knew he was both foreman and worker, and they were depending on him to finish the job. His first thought was along the same lines: How was he going to finish the kitchen backsplash?

With personal concerns aside, however, his injury's effect on our company became an immediate issue. Because he was a highly skilled and knowledgeable employee and a crucial part of our business success, we all wondered how this was going to affect company growth.

Like most new business owners, I had no idea how important it was to document the underlying processes that made my company tick. On the surface, I could see that we were profitable. I understood what we did and why, so it seemed fair to assume I also knew the everyday minutiae backing my company's success.

But as soon as he told me he was going to be out of the office for a while, some serious questions hung over me: *Do I (or anyone else, for that matter) even know everything his job entails? How will we function without him? Who will fill his responsibilities? Should I hire a short-term replacement or ask other employees to step up their involvement?*

He had a great deal of autonomy in his role, so I really didn't know much about his day-to-day responsibilities. One day I was a CEO guiding my ship through calm waters. The next day we hit an iceberg, and I needed to join the crew as we bailed buckets of water from the hull to prevent capsizing.

We had recently completed a project with our largest client to date, so business was a little slow, and the stakes were higher than ever. I immediately went into action trying to uncover every one of his tasks that needed completion. "Overwhelmed" doesn't begin to describe my feeling about the situation. I know business owners are supposed to operate as if nobody is irreplaceable, but at that moment, I felt he was an exception to the rule. His absence plunged me into a dual mode of full-time employer and employee. I was frantically fighting to be two people at once, handicapped by the fact that we were new enough not to have developed meaningful job descriptions. We were still making it up as we went along and hadn't captured our "best practices" on paper.

 In a time of crisis we all have the potential to morph up to a new level and do things we never thought possible. —Stuart Wilde

He was out of the office for a while. Once he returned healthy—and having survived my attempt at doing his job—I had room to breathe and fully examine what had occurred. A broken bone uncovered a fracture in my company, what some might call a "single point of failure." A single point of failure is basically the one part of a system that, if broken, can stop the entire system from working at all. This can come in many forms—from a key employee's absence to the bank tightening credit, from an unexpected lawsuit to a force of nature. In other words, it's any single event or dynamic that could take down your business in one fell swoop. The most common single point of failure in a start-up is you, the founder and owner. As we recovered from the negative impact of a key employee's misfortune, I knew I could never let this upheaval happen again if it was preventable.

Looking for the Weak Links

When you are a company's founder, looking objectively at your own business is difficult. Criticism of it feels like criticism of your own child. Anticipating the future is even more difficult. But in order to become a platform-driven business, searching for weaknesses is a crucial step. No one wanted to hear the British host announce, "You are the weakest link. Good-bye," on a popular TV show that used to air. And no one likes to hear their weaknesses paraded for all to see.

But wanting to strengthen my business and create more stability for times of crisis, I knew it was time for a calculated plan of action in my enterprise. With guidance from my advisory board, I began analyzing our weak points. While doing so, I discovered a very important operational flaw. My employees did not have written job descriptions, so no one had a concrete understanding of their own, much less their colleagues', roles. Without documented processes and responsibilities, a company's growth is limited because best practices and industry knowledge are lost with employee turnover. If I really wanted to mature into a platform company, we couldn't afford to have one employee's presence or absence (even my own) determine our success.

Thus began the laborious, yearlong task of creating institutionalized processes, job descriptions, and HR procedures. Research consistently shows that tying compensation to achievement will result in greater effort and engagement. So we decided to design a certification process for all employees. We came up with a multistep personal and professional development program that allowed every employee the opportunity for career advancement, and increased salary based on completing progressive certifications. Upon implementing the program, we were able to eliminate not just that flaw, but several points of failure. By examining each individual role and responsibility and building a development system that highlights and improves performance in these areas, we saw multiplied benefits to our investment.

It worked. The process was put to the test when my mother was sick for six months before she passed away. During her illness, I became a ghost of myself at work; while I was physically in the office, mentally I was absent. But because we had put in the effort to build a platform on which to run the company, I had the freedom to mourn and be less than my best without losing my business.

And as captain of the ship, I no longer needed to keep buckets beside my desk in case a new leak had sprung. It was at this point in the development of the business that I began to understand the concept of creating a company versus creating a job for myself.

Growing Up as a Company and CEO

I hope I never trade building enterprises for a dull, ho-hum job. That's why I took the entrepreneurial road. That's why you're reading this book too. But just like moving from the teen years and assuming grown-up responsibilities, your business needs to grow up too.

The maturation of a business isn't to be taken lightly, and the task isn't for everyone. Maybe your *modus operandi* is to build it and sell before it gets too big—and repeat the process. That's good. But the long-term benefits of performance analysis are clear: a platform company holds much greater value and lasting potential than any sole proprietorship ever can. I took the risk to start my own company because I wanted autonomy and to reap the rewards that came with knowing I was responsible for my own performance and success. But as we grew, I came to understand the reality that no single person should be the make-or-break point in an organization. Many entrepreneurs struggle with this; the transition from actively participating in every aspect of the business's day-to-day functioning to stepping back and building the systems where others hold key responsibilities can be rocky. A lot of people like the idea of being a CEO but fail to realize that the actual demands of leadership include careful planning for one's own absence and boring things like paperwork and documentation—and, of course, a continued willingness to jump in and get any job done if a single point of failure occurs. It is your company, after all.

SWOT Analysis

Periodically, you need to measure what is happening inside and outside your company. One of the simplest methods, SWOT Analysis, was developed by Albert Humphries and introduced at Stanford University in the 1960s.

Look at the following chart and make a list under each heading to gain insights on ways you can improve strategic plans to keep your company healthy.

	Strengths	**Weaknesses**
Internal		
External	**Opportunities**	**Threats**

Giving up control of daily responsibilities is frightening, but being the only person who knows the complete company structure is a much scarier prospect. I have read countless books outlining what to do and when, but no hypothetical advice can uncover every aspect of a company's needs and shortcomings. Looking objectively for flaws that you can't cover yourself and then systematically eliminating them through good planning and system takes time, toil, and a willingness to challenge something you want to believe is perfect. The good news is that this doesn't happen all at once. You don't wear five hats one day and then suddenly remove all of them to simply manage. It's usually one hat at a time. You figure out how the role or task can be done just as well or better without you. You build the protocol, and you take off the hat to concentrate on your next area that needs improvement.

How you delegate will determine the rate at which your venture grows. In a bedtime story from *Aesop's Fables,* a shepherd had more sheep in his flock than he could care for by himself. A particularly sly wolf noted this and started coming around each day, not to attack the sheep, but to help the shepherd keep them fed, watered, and safely together—much like a sheepherding dog would do. The shepherd was amazed at this surprising turn of events, though he was still quite wary of this most unlikely source of help. But over time, he let his defenses down, until one day he felt free to go to town for supplies—and leave the sheep in the care of the wolf. When he returned that night, to his dismay, his flock was scattered, and almost half had become dinner for animals of prey.

The wise entrepreneur deals with delegation issues in a timely fashion so that he doesn't find himself in a desperate situation where he has to depend on wolves to keep his business fed, watered, and running.

The Moral of the Story

In the early days of a start-up, everything depends on you. In order to mature as a CEO and as a company, you must build systems that allow the company to succeed without you or any other single person.

For Reflection and Action

1. Are you running a business, or have you created a job for yourself?

2. How do you end your involvement in day-to-day responsibilities without harming the company?

3. What are your first steps in discovering your company's single points of failure?

4. Do your employees have written, up-to-date job descriptions? Are you capable of stepping in or filling any opening that may suddenly occur?

5. Are there any employees whose departure would destroy your company?

Chapter 8
DON'T CUT CORNERS

It's not enough that we do our best; sometimes we have to do what's required.

—Sir Winston Churchill

AN EXECUTIVE SEARCH IS CHALLENGING. Like panning for gold in a river, you have to sift through a lot of rubble before you find something valuable. Then there's always the possibility that what you thought was treasure is nothing more than fool's gold.

In my line of work, I often find it helpful to work with partners. One in particular runs a firm in San Jose that specializes in senior level financial executives. Steve, the owner, and I were catching up one day, and during our conversation, he asked me if I had time for a story. I said yes, and he shared an experience that is a real nightmare in my industry. It cemented in my mind that we had better keep doing the little things we have done to become successful if we want to keep things that way. Skipping steps can be detrimental to a company's health.

Searching for Jane S.

When he started his firm, he was doing all the selling and recruiting himself. His business was young, and he knew one significant placement would really put him on the map. One of his earliest opportunities came when a major company tapped him to fill a highly specialized financial management opening.

His was one of two agencies entrusted to find the right executive. This important opportunity wasn't all that random—he had previously worked for the executive who needed to fill the open position. He knew the boss, what this person liked and didn't like, and he felt like this was a race he could win. He was also flattered that his former boss thought highly of his skills and believed he was capable of finding the right person for this job. The task at hand was no small feat, and this client was no start-up. This was the real deal, a reference account that people would actually notice. He knew that his success would open the door to a lot more business.

With the pressure on, he embarked on the search to end all searches. To say there was a limited number of people who fit the company's requirements would be a gross understatement. The position required not only a track record of excellent performance, but highly specific customer knowledge and industry experience. Ready for the challenge, he began combing résumés and making phone calls to his network of people, who supplied him referrals. But the specific combination of industry competency and experience made finding the right person tougher than hunting Tom Turkey on Thanksgiving morning. He looked for weeks.

After a coast-to-coast search for any person who might possess the demanding skill set, he narrowed the list down to the top ten candidates. In submitting his preliminary findings to a client, he didn't want to waste anyone's time, so only the applicants who he believed fully and exactly matched the position's qualifications would be presented. After carefully weeding through the remaining résumés one more time, he was left with one single person who fit the requirement: Jane S. She was spot-on in every qualification.

I am careful not to confuse excellence
with perfection. Excellence, I can reach
for; perfection is God's business.
—Michael J. Fox

After interviewing Jane and talking to her references, he felt incredibly optimistic that she would be hired. She performed outstandingly in her interview, and her résumé was immaculate. He knew she was a perfect fit for the hardest placement he'd ever attempted. He was pumped and felt an incredible sense of accomplishment. He was ready to pop the cork on the champagne and start celebrating the next phase of his business before he even sent her information to the client. He presented her résumé and history to the executive in charge of hires and waited for their appreciative return call.

Stop the Presses

Stop the presses. Put on the brakes. Don't pop the cork just yet.

The response from the client was not what Steve had expected. Rather than announcing how perfect Jane S. was for the job, he received an e-mail with the subject line, "Who is the real Jane S.?"

Huh?

Intrigued (and a little anxious), he opened the message to find two attachments and no note. Both files were résumés for Jane S. One was his and the other was sent in by Steve's competitor. Now, it is highly unusual for two firms to submit the same candidate for a position. One of his responsibilities as a recruiter was to know where candidates have applied in their job search. Somehow, though, his due diligence failed. This small detail about Jane S. slipped through the cracks. But that's not all. As the infomercial ads say, "But wait, there's more."

Steve had a much more sobering realization. This mishap was more than sloppy research or an odd coincidence. Comparing the two résumés, he discovered that the names matched, the addresses matched, and the phone numbers matched, but that was it. The employment histories were completely different. The résumé he submitted showed Jane S. working at ABC Consulting from 1994 to 1998; the résumé the competitor submitted listed her employment at XYZ Consulting during the same period. You would never believe both résumés belonged to the same woman. He was floored. Embarrassed. Disappointed. And mad as hell. He'd been duped. How could he be so stupid?

 I think it's very important that whatever you're trying to make or sell, or teach has to be basically good. A bad product, and you know what? You won't be here in ten years. —Martha Stewart

In trying to reassure himself that this wasn't entirely his fault, he looked back at the vetting process he had gone through to even consider Jane S. as the number one applicant. He knew he diligently contacted and approved her references. That step was not neglected. He also knew the other recruiting firm. It was a high-quality, trustworthy business opponent of his, similarly focused on doing good work. During the whole hiring process, Jane seemed competent and legitimate and provided thoughtful answers to any question he had thrown at her. What he failed to realize ahead of time was that while she expressed an air of confidence based on experience, Jane had purposefully set up different references for every fake job on her résumés. With these positive referrals, Jane S. seemed even more like his Triple Crown winner. Instead, she turned out to be the Trojan horse, appearing as a gift in order to get inside his city and wreak havoc. Both firms had fallen hook, line, and sinker for her lies.

Thankfully, the client actually found the mix-up amusing. Steve spent time with the client explaining how the mistake was made and discussed additional steps he would add to his own vetting process to make this a blue moon occurrence—though not impossible for a professional con artist. Maybe it was because he had a past relationship with the client, or maybe it was just his honesty of admitting he screwed up. Bottom line: He fell on the sword of ego and then explained how he was going to be better next time, and that kept him in the client's good graces. The last time we chatted—and I always ask—he told me he continues to work with the client and their relationship is stronger then ever.

Small Mistakes, Big Consequences

Okay, good story. Honest mistake. Happens to the best of them. What does this have to do with being an entrepreneur? Sometimes the smallest mistakes have the biggest consequences. As entrepreneurs, we are pulled in many different directions simultaneously. Decisions are made very quickly. Most of the time, we make the right call, but sometimes we fail because we have gotten sloppy and not kept up the habits that made us successful in the first place. Like the scenario where Steve ended up with egg on his face, one missed step scuttles hours of work. This situation could have been easily resolved with a quick verification of employment dates. He didn't check. He should have. He made no excuses for that. And he ended up spinning his wheels on a project with no payout.

You might be expecting a pep talk at this point: Go above and beyond what is expected; deliver extraordinary service; do the exceptional. Sounds like good business practice to me. But my point is not for you to do the extraordinary, but rather to do the required. When your own money is on the line, due diligence means checking additional references and verifying dates, *every single time,* no matter how much you like or trust someone. Gut feelings are crucial, but so is hard evidence.

This Is a Football

A bedtime story is told about legendary NFL football Coach Vince Lombardi. If his Packers lost or didn't play to the level he thought they should, he would begin the next practice by holding up a football and telling the team, "This is a football." He might then walk through fundamentals like blocking and tackling and holding a football correctly, as if he were coaching a peewee football team made up of ten-year-olds. He was never known as the flashiest or most creative coach. But his teams played sound, hard-nosed football. Every game. And they won almost all of them.

Going to the Dogs

The president of a dog food company hosted an all company meeting. To generate enthusiasm and participation, he called out a series of questions and asked for everyone to call out the answer together.

Who has the best-looking dog food packaging? "We do," the crowd shouted back to him.

Who has the most award-winning commercials on TV? "We do," the crowd roared.

Who has the grandest international headquarters? "We do," the employees yelled even louder.

Who has the most technologically advanced production techniques? "We do!" came back in a near frenzy.

Then why aren't we selling more dog food? The meeting room went deathly silent as the CEO scanned the room.

Finally, a shy, little man who worked on the assembly line stood up. Everyone looked at him.

"Because the dogs won't eat it, sir," he called out.

No matter how many things you do well, beware of that one thing that will still rob you of success.

If you're blowing and going and growing, it might be time to slow down and make sure you're holding the football right.

People—though not everyone—lie on their résumés all the time, and if someone can become a Division I football coach or CEO of a major corporation or a candidate for political office with a falsified résumé, who's to say your candidates aren't attempting the same? That's my world. Yours is much different. But the principle of taking care of the fundamentals is the same.

The Moral of the Story

To grow a company, you must have salesmanship and be able to market the sizzle. But your ongoing success will always be tied to executing the fundamentals with excellence.

For Reflection and Action

1. What are the fundamentals of your business?

2. What are the consequences of cutting corners when you get "caught"?

3. Have you developed a written system—even if it's just a checklist—to make sure you do the job right?

4. How can you communicate your commitment to doing things right to your customers and make this part of your value proposition?

Chapter 9

DON'T TRY TO DO EVERYTHING

Doing a job badly and then getting someone in to sort it out can be much more expensive than getting someone in to do the job properly in the first place.

—Sarah Beeny

YOU KNOW THOSE NOW-UBIQUITOUS MASTERCARD commercials that tabulate the costs for activities that create a priceless experience? If I had to write the script of what is priceless for a small business owner, it would go something like this:

Best attorney you can afford: $$

Banker whose service is so good you pay the fees without negotiating: $$$

Accountant who gets it right the first time: $$

Controller who shows you when to make a move to avoid a future problem: $$$

Having the freedom to advance your business by leveraging the strengths that made you successful: priceless

Now, imagine every company you've ever worked for. How many of these businesses hired one individual to serve as an accountant, controller, banker, head of sales, attorney, and IT professional? I'd be willing to bet the answer is none of them. But building a profitable company often leaves start-up entrepreneurs trying to juggle a variety of responsibilities. Too many responsibilities. Some they are lousy at.

In the early days of my start-up, I managed every aspect of the company. Sure, I could brag about how hard I worked, but the reality is that I was feeling completely overwhelmed and stressed by the mountain of work piling up—both the variety and sheer number of tasks. In the back of my mind, I knew I couldn't manage it all. The more I attempted to micromanage, the more frustrated and weighed down I became. I spent countless nights lying awake, wondering whether I had recklessly put my future and my family's well-being on the line. The problem was that outsourcing every service I needed was not a feasible option when I considered the impact on the bottom line and the checkbook balance. In time, though, I realized I stood to lose more by not bringing in at least some outside experts.

As a CEO, I excel at vision, leadership, and sales. As you picked up on earlier, I'm not great with spreadsheets. I don't know a lot about banking. I definitely don't hold a J.D. Eventually, I realized that being the Superman Business Owner doesn't bring your company success. As the "jack of all trades, master of none" cliché illustrates, you can't be the best in every area at once. And that's okay. Rarely can a single individual do everything at once, do it well, and still have a personal life. Here are the basic functions you need covered.

The Banker

The importance of having a strong banking relationship was wisdom passed down from my father, a successful businessman. He taught me that for a company the size of mine, it is crucial to build a relationship with a locally owned bank instead of one of the enormous brand-name institutions. National banks have an impressive number of accounts to manage, and a growing company can easily become just another number. My dad pointed out to me that not only can small, community-focused banks personally service your account, they also need your business just as much as you need their services. Think George Bailey and Bedford Falls in *It's a Wonderful Life*. Actively invested in your success, smaller institutions tend to offer more flexibility, frequently lending start-ups more money and providing better service options than the big guys.

After running into a few brick walls with a very large institution, I followed my father's advice and began maintaining my operating accounts with local and regional banks. Because my banker represents an independent financial institution, I never quibble about pricing. I understand that their success depends upon the success of our relationship. Consequently, I want my banker to make money so they are on my side of the table. Together, we help ensure that both of our companies profit. It's a perfect example of "you scratch my back, and I'll scratch yours."

One of the key services a banker can provide is a line of credit secured by your accounts receivable. At a point when my company wasn't performing so well, my banker informed me that she believed one of my receivables was not valuable and she could not lend money against it. Honestly, I wasn't completely surprised by this downgrade. I had recently questioned whether the client would be able to pay us. Hoping I was just being overly anxious, I hadn't acted on my suspicions. After all, we really needed the money.

Unfortunately at the time—yet fortunately for the future— my banker's lack of confidence confirmed my doubts. The truth was that we were experiencing financial trouble from a company with a possible bankruptcy looming in its future. That troublesome news played over and over again in my mind. I lost sleep wondering whether the client would be able to pay me. So when I addressed the issue with my banker, her informed input as to my risk level made me realize that I needed to move quickly to resolve the situation. I changed my strategy with the client and received payment for all invoices in question. Had I waited another couple of months, I would have received nothing. Our financial standing immediately became less stressful.

Now, had my banker not personally looked out for my company's well-being, in this case pushing for a decisive, timely action, I might have been even more negatively impacted by what eventually ended in a bankruptcy. And while my banker is definitely not the cheapest option around, her competence is worth every penny I pay for her services. I greatly value and benefit from her personal attentiveness to my company's success. Her interest and dedication have saved me much more money than any APR drop ever could.

The Accountant

I haven't always outsourced services with the right motivation. At the time we hired our accountants, I was greatly concerned about the company's escalating costs. Like most business owners, I was looking for anyplace to trim our expenses. We decided a smart way to start was choosing accountants that were less expensive than the premier firms in the industry. It was worth it to save a little more money.

Or so we thought.

The first year the accountants did our taxes, I was happy to receive a small amount of money back, but couldn't escape the nagging feeling something wasn't right. While I'm not an accounting whiz, my gut kept telling me there was a problem with this firm. And it didn't help that whenever my advisory board asked questions about the books, I couldn't provide the right answers. "Something looks off," they kept telling me. "Figures seem to be in the wrong columns." At that point, I really didn't understand all of the intricacies of financial statements, and I couldn't explain if the firm's accounting was creative or just plain incorrect. The more the board inquired, the less I felt I knew. But I knew something wasn't adding up.

When you've hired people to make sure *everything* adds up correctly, it's an overwhelming feeling to think they've erroneously calculated and assigned your numbers. After careful consideration and repeated inquiries from my board, I decided to test the accountants' ability against my gut instinct. I knew I wouldn't be able to uncover any problems myself, so I hired a separate accounting firm to double-check the paperwork. It turned out my gut was right. Okay, to be honest, it was my advisory board that was right. The books were completely off, and consequently, my tax returns were wrong. I had no other choice but to refile with the IRS.

What started as a brilliant plan to save money with a cheaper firm resulted in paying twice as much for the same service. In anger, I sent our first accounting firm an invoice for the second accountant's bill. Up to this point in our relationship, they returned my calls promptly and frequently. But this time around, not surprisingly, they never got back to me. In fact, I never heard from the accountants again. My company ended up footing the bill for their mistakes. A costly lesson to learn, yes, but one that we will never have to repeat just because we're trying to save a little money.

The Controller

In the early days of my business, we hired a top-notch business consultant to create an intricate web of lever-driven data, not realizing how hard it would be to interpret. I used to spend hours each week wrestling with spreadsheets, trying to determine how specific choices would affect the company. With each potential decision, I would filter, flow, and sort the outcome. I knew the answers were hidden in the documents, but all the snake charming I could muster wouldn't coax them out.

There are risks and costs to a program
of action, but they are far less than
the long-range risks and costs of
comfortable inaction. —John F.
Kennedy

Understanding my spreadsheet shortcomings, one of my advisory board members had been urging me to hire a controller for several years, someone who could contribute the skills I lacked to our growing company. I was frustrated that I couldn't decipher the numbers, but I didn't believe I could justify the cost. And I continued needing answers to my what-ifs: *What if we spend more money on marketing? What if we hire a new employee? What if we let an employee go?* These matters were urgent.

After several failed attempts, I realized I couldn't find the answers on my own—no matter how many times I tried. I was wasting an incredible amount of time bouncing around the spreadsheets, retrieving none of the information I needed. With my patience waning, my temper on edge, and with answers still proving elusive, I finally took the board's advice and hired a controller to read the massive amount of information and distill it for my use. I'd already learned the hard way what happens when I cut the wrong corner, so this time around, I hired someone who had the professional skills to back up a much higher price tag than I wanted to pay, but who could get the job done right. My company certainly wasn't profiting from my attempts at this data mining, so the skills of a professional were worth the cost.

Information is power because it gives us a stronger base from which to make better decisions. The controller retrieved my much-needed data immediately. Some of it I didn't even know existed or never would have asked for on my own. She was able to provide accurate, updated, and simple answers I could use every week to make better decisions. Subsequently, my frustration calmed. I realized biting the bullet and leveraging the skills of another person enabled me to hit the bull's eye with one succinct punch. I could now move forward and make the necessary decisions for continuing to build my company's success. And yes, I also realized I better hear and heed the guidance of my advisory board. They are my *advisory* board, after all.

Pay or Pain

The preceding three examples represent the pay-or-pain effect. When I've chosen to hire the best people I can afford, only positive outcomes have resulted. I am able to focus on my strengths, generate growth, actively save money, and put my effort into building a stronger future. On the contrary, whenever I've tried to scrimp on services, I've lost time and peace, put my business in jeopardy, and ended up spending more money than if I'd hired or outsourced properly skilled professionals in the first place.

My experience confirms that all business is supply and demand. The professionals who command higher prices are usually able to do so because they are more skilled than their cheaper competitors. Just as a Bentley costs more than a Kia, there's a reason some business professionals cost more than others. There are certainly bankers, accountants, and controllers who are less expensive than the individuals I've hired, and maybe some that are more expensive, but I've purposefully chosen the best professionals I can afford and have built long-term relationships with them. By efficiently providing a specific and needed service, they have allowed me to streamline my own responsibilities. I now handle only the ones in which I excel—and that alone is worth every cent.

Besides hiring and outsourcing, one other option you can consider to deliver excellent services and expanded capacity is forming partnerships, joint ventures, or some other form of strategic alliance. In the simplest of terms, this can be thought of as 1 + 1 = 3 or synergy with complimentary companies. My own experience in forming partnerships has not been universally successful. I just gave one example of why it is important to form a strategic alliance in the first place; you have a client who needs something that they can provide better than you, and you trust that partner enough that you're willing to share fees without fear of losing the customer. In many cases, either my interests or my partner's interest had too much overlap and did not provide a successful solution for the client.

In the cases where successful partnerships have been established, I have noticed several similarities for a win-win partnership—equal commitment to the same level of service; the services are more complimentary than competitive; each partner does something more often and better than the other partner; high levels of trust; both partners win, but ultimately, the customer is the bigger winner.

You Can't Do Everything

The entire livelihood of a start-up company is built on its founder. But to become a *successful* business owner, it is your responsibility to accept that you can't do it all. If you genuinely want to go from a sole proprietorship to a platform company, you must go beyond daily concerns and minutiae to create the vision and do the planning that will take you there. To do so, you must identify the skills you have and determine where you add the most value to your company. It might help to consider where you excelled in your career before starting a business. Then, as your budget allows, pay the best professionals to handle every other aspect.

That doesn't mean emptying your checkbook on non-strategic functions or on areas you already have covered. The question is the simple cost-benefit ratio. The more benefit a function provides, the more important it is.

When was the last time you paid too much for something of very high quality? For me, the answer is never. As a small business owner, I know how tempting (and futile) it is to try to save your way to prosperity. Working with limited capital is always challenging. When it's your own money rather than your employer's, you're dealing with a whole new set of pressures and frustrations. I think it's natural to question which expenditures are crucial and which can wait—that's a part of the daily responsibilities in owning a company. The risk comes when you try to reduce costs by morphing into The Business Owner Who Does It All and consequently does nothing right or well. As I've said before, you must fight the solitary nature of business ownership by entrusting yourself to a group of professionals who can relate to your challenges and make recommendations. From fellow business owners to mentors, use your network to get referrals before hiring anyone, and trust your gut once you do.

The Bill Gates Plan

On January 13, 2000, Bill Gates, CEO of Microsoft and the wealthiest man in the world, announced that he was stepping down as chief executive of the company he founded and handing over the reins to Steve Ballmer, his best friend and longtime right-hand man.

The business community was in shock. Was Gates sick? Had the long, arduous battle with the U.S. Department of Justice over antitrust suits finally worn him out?

As the media dug into the story, the answer had been right in front of them for a couple of years. All that time, Gates had been telling anyone that would listen that Ballmer had as much authority and equally shared the top spot at Microsoft. His transition into a more active product development role had been in the works the whole time.

But why let loose of the top spot? Gates felt he could better serve Microsoft in technology, and he felt Ballmer was a better CEO than he was—a lesson to the wise from one of the most successful entrepreneurs in human history.

It's impossible to be gifted in every area of business—just as it's impossible to be an expert on everything. We all have different gifts and strengths. There's a legend that tells of a beautiful horse that wanted to be even more impressive and praiseworthy. It called out to the creator and asked that he grant his wish to improve on his already handsome looks. The god encouraged him to be comfortable with who he was, but after some argument, he agreed to do as the horse requested and followed his instructions exactly. When the transformed horse looked at his reflection in a clear pool, to his horror, he discovered that the god had turned him into a camel. He bitterly complained and asked to be made into a horse again, but the god told him he had to live with the changes as punishment for not being grateful for the way he had created him in the first place. He said to the horse: "If you cry for a longer neck and legs, this is what will happen. Each thing in my creation has its own good qualities. The camel is not as beautiful as you are, but it carries heavy loads and has a tremendous sense of responsibility."

Sometimes the entrepreneur is forced to be all things to all people. And it's true, we can grow into new roles and responsibilities. But when we focus our time—and money—to hone our own strengths and honor the strengths of others, we ensure that the group functions and performs better.

The Moral of the Story

You can't be an expert on everything. You need to strategically hire—or outsource—in ways that maximize your strengths and compensate for your weaknesses.

For Reflection and Action

1. What are your strengths? Your weaknesses? This may seem basic, but it's good to periodically take inventory.

2. Does your company's success hinge on areas where you are weak or strong?

3. How easily do you delegate? As a business owner, do you feel like you should be able to perform every function needed in your company?

4. What tasks can you relinquish now or in the coming months to improve your company's performance?

5. Do you have trusted peers or mentors who will point out your weaknesses and recommend solutions?

Chapter 10

DON'T RELY ON ONE CUSTOMER

I N A SENSE, STARTING YOUR own company means you are not diversifying, but are investing in a single stock—belief in yourself. I applaud the courage that it takes and have followed the same path myself. Now it's time to return to diversification as an investment model by building your customer base.

My wife and I met a couple at a charity function, and the four of us hit it off right away. The husband was part of a company that was in the start-up phase of building an advertising firm. I was a little further in the process of establishing a viable business, so he asked if we could meet at Starbucks so he and a partner could pick my brain on some of the challenges they were facing. I love to share anything I can offer to other entrepreneurs. I also know that whatever I share with others comes back to me in the form of new insights for my own business. And that proved to be the case on this rainy Saturday morning over a steaming cup of hot coffee.

Sometimes It's Low Tide. Right?

My new friend and his partner were in an advertising business that was doing pretty well. They had a client who represented nearly 50 percent of their revenue and 85 percent of their accounts receivable. Their accounts receivable that month were $300,000; this client represented approximately $255,000 of that total. To make the situation even more pressing, they had already incurred costs of $180,000 out of their own line of credit—all the while accruing interest, of course. Further complicating their situation was that they did not have direct access to the end client; they were working through a third-party prime contractor. They were a subcontractor, yet had full financial responsibility to pay their people, and the prime contractor was only obligated to pay them once the job was done and he himself was paid. Unfortunately, those payments were coming slower and slower. These two guys used to get paid every thirty days, but it had started slipping to ninety.

They were becoming uncomfortable with the relationship, but they were a relatively new company and were pretty happy to have the work. They figured slow payments and multitiered pay arrangements were part of doing business. They had decided not to worry about the potential problems with their situation, holding to the belief that everything would work itself out. After all, cash flow was just that: flow. Sometimes the tide is high, sometimes it's lower than normal—particularly during certain phases of the moon, right? Besides, they felt they were really in their element and believed their business was headed in the right direction. It's what they were good at. They were hired by this intermediary firm because of their ability to do their job well. So they decided they would ride out the difficulties.

Over the course of their short, but robust, relationship, the prime contractor did some things that raised serious red flags. Remember that out-of-control accounts receivable? That proved to be just the tip of the iceberg. Meanwhile, their own bills remained unpaid.

The week before I sat down with them at Starbucks, they got a call to meet with the intermediary firm. They thought this would be a good opportunity to address the payment problem, as well as some other issues that were giving them heartburn. Instead, they learned that the end client wanted a reduction in rates, justified by how much business he was sending their way. The fledgling company would have to absorb this reduction. Making this expo-nentially more uncomfortable was the fact that they still had no direct contact with the client. In fact, they were contractually prohibited from having any financial discussions with them.

Firing a Large Client—and Lessons Learned

These actions seemed particularly brazen in a market where these guys believed that they were one of the very few local firms that could successfully provide the solution that the intermediary firm—and thus the client—needed to successfully open a new market. They pointed this out in the meeting. Their contact agreed with them—but said there was nothing he could do about it. So during a meeting that they thought was going to solve problems, they made the very painful decision to "fire" their biggest customer. As they told me the story, I thought to myself, *This could happen to anyone. This could happen to me.*

It happens every day. Entrepreneurs go out to start a business and actually get a client. They are so pumped to have that client that they focus on delivering quality work and simply assume the money will roll in equal to the quality and quantity of their work. Often it does. But they still face a risk. The day could come when they wake up and watch that client walk away and their entire business with it.

That day, those two gentlemen came to me for some advice, and I hope I gave them some. But they presented me with two very valuable lessons, ones that ended up helping me not just avoid catastrophe, but actually *grow* my business. First, as a result of our conversation, my company now has in place specific guidelines about how we source and engage potential clients. In our new world, no single client will ever account for more than 25 percent of our business. Secondly, we adopted the practice of always striving to operate in multiple industries. It's a precarious balance of objectives: You start a business because you're good at something, and that something may be really relevant and applicable to one industry—but you also have to work to keep those strengths flexible and applicable to multiple industries in order to prevent the challenges that come from overly relying on one area of business. These days, you'll find my company working in health care, technology, government, and financial services. We also hope to extend our reach to government contracts to further recession-proof our business.

Finding the Right Mix of Customers

In a start-up, nothing is more important to an entrepreneur than a first customer. Those first clients might not be the greatest, but they're absolutely necessary. But I've found that start-up business owners need to continually monitor not only the quality of their relationships with clients and customer service, but also the diversity of their client portfolios. Whether you like what you see or not, you need to take a good hard look at your client base. If you choose to depend on a small number of clients for a large percentage of your revenue, you're making a decision that could have serious consequences.

 Intelligent media companies strive to provide both intellectual and comedy programs, groundbreaking and reflective articles, art house and popular movies. Not to be open-minded in providing a full range of quality media would be a failure to serve the breadth and depth of the communities we live in. —Lachlan Murdoch

Decisions between risk and reward are a part of everyday life for entrepreneurs. The problem with the scenario these two gentlemen discussed was that they lacked the experience and foresight to see the grave risk in their situation. In the early days of my own company, I had no active strategy to diversify because I was too busy working *in* the business than working *on* the business. But I've learned my lesson. As easy as it may be to concentrate your efforts on one client who pays big, the risk almost always outweighs the reward if it means you're dependent on that single account.

Everyone wants to be as lucky as the simpleton in the Grimm Brothers' tale who found a goose that laid golden eggs. We all love the idea of a neat, simple way to "make rain." The start-up CEO needs to know that the real danger isn't him or her killing the hen that lays golden eggs—but having her turn on you!

Double Vision

The best entrepreneurs have "double vision."

- Their eyes are fixed on the present—and they see the future at the same time.

- They see their favorite client right in front of them—and they see all their other clients the same way.

- They see their biggest customer and realize how fortunate they are—and they see their smaller customers and realize how much potential for growth there is.

The Moral of the Story

If you become dependent on very few customers, losing even one or two can jeopardize your enterprise. You must diversify.

For Reflection and Action

1. What percentage of your business do your three largest clients represent?

2. How are these clients doing financially in the current market? How would your business be affected if your largest client suddenly declared bankruptcy?

3. You should have diverse customers; do your clients? Do you know?

4. Do you have excessive exposure in any one sector of the economy?

5. What are three action steps you need to establish in order to diversify?

Chapter 11

DON'T BE A SCROOGE

> In business, you're trying to make a buck. God was good to me and blessed me. I made some money and started this foundation years ago, and it has grown in size. With the foundation it's a lot different, because the bottom line isn't how you can make more money or get a better return, it's helping the projects that you feel strongly about move forward.
>
> —Lee Iacocca

I N 2004, I DECIDED TO make charitable giving a solid part of our culture. It wasn't strategy, passion, or even tax planning that sparked the idea. It was running.

The idea came to me when I decided to join a marathon training group. I ran one marathon in 2001, but without a regular running program, I was gaining another ten or fifteen pounds every few years. In my younger days, I used to be able to eat and drink what I wanted and maintain a consistent weight. I'm sure you know what aging does to that freedom. Now I wanted to get back in shape. I wasn't motivated enough to prepare for another marathon on my own, so I decided to join a local training team. I thought it would be a good opportunity to get professional running guidance and meet new people who were similarly driven by high-octane pursuits. But in the end, I got a lot more out of it than some pleasant camaraderie, a slimmer waistline, a sense of accomplishment, and a better race time.

The Fellowship of the Runners

Any marathoner can attest to the fact that long runs have a way of stripping away superficiality in conversations. When you pound the pavement for hours, gasping for air alongside complete strangers, you really get to know your training partners. One of the runners in my group was the manager of Comfort Zone Camp, a local nonprofit. Over many miles (and buckets of sweat) he told me all about his organization. I felt an immediate emotional reaction to his story, which was surprising considering it was all I could do to keep breathing.

Comfort Zone Camp supports the emotional needs of children who have lost a parent, sibling, or primary caregiver. It provides a free camp where these children are allowed the rare opportunity to grieve openly in a safe, supportive, and constructive environment. The more this man described the life-changing effects Comfort Zone Camp had on these children, the more I wanted to help. Thoughts of my own sons and daughter and how they would respond if they lost my wife or me deepened my connection to this cause, and I grew determined to become a supporter. I liked that it was a local program, offering services to suffering children in my community, and I had a ton of confidence and trust in one of the key people working with Comfort Zone Camp. The gears in my mind kept turning. No longer concerned with the many miles left to run, my only focus now was the drive I felt to support this group.

Because I had young children at home, the requirements of volunteering meant it wasn't feasible for me to provide on-site help, but I knew my company could write a check. This would not be the first nonprofit organization to which we had donated a substantial amount of money, but this time my sense of responsibility to do so felt different. More than a year-end check, I was ready to establish a philanthropic relationship.

There was good response inside my company when I presented the idea, and we began sponsoring the annual black-tie Grief Relief Gala. We all invited our network of friends and associates. Although this initial sponsorship required a substantial donation for a company our size, it was the beginning of a nonprofit focus that now means a great deal to me and my employees.

After seeing the positive impact we could have on Comfort Zone Camp, I realized personal and professional success is defined by more than just money and lifestyle. Real success is also defined by the extent to which we are able and willing to give back to those in need. I believe it is a business owner's responsibility to uplift and support the community that has given so much to him or her.

As a company, we developed a commitment to choosing worthwhile causes and supporting them with ongoing donations. Because several core members of my team also had young families, we tended to focus on groups meeting the needs of children. We added the Make-a-Wish Foundation to our ongoing efforts. We have subsequently added the Children's Home Society, which finds homes for children; Operation Warm, a group providing coats in the winter for children whose families can't afford them; and the Fanconi Anemia Research Fund, a nonprofit supporting research for the genetic disease Fanconi anemia, which occurs in babies born with a missing chromosome, who then face devastating and often life-threatening challenges as they approach adulthood.

Put to the Test—An Uphill Climb

In the years since our first Grief Relief Gala, we have donated more than 7.5 percent of our net profits to local charitable organizations. As our company has grown, our donations have increased proportionately. We felt pride and were pleased to substantially help these organizations succeed, because success isn't fully achieved unless you can share it with others.

Then came 2007.

It wasn't a great year for the company in terms of profit and loss. A rocky expansion effort had us hemorrhaging cash. We were having to make cost-cutting decisions in the same way a family would have to cut back on activities and extras during a financial hardship. Toughest of all, we had to make the difficult decision to prioritize which causes to support and to what degree we could afford to support them. We did make the commitment to keep our percentage of giving at 7.5 percent of our profits. But it was significantly fewer dollars. We still wanted our donations to have a measurable impact on the organizations with the most immediate needs. Choosing between good or better—needy or needier—is never easy. Throughout the course of our involvement with these organizations, many of them felt like a part of our corporate family. But with our cash flow in a crunch, the decision had to be made.

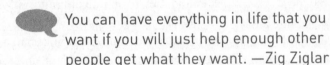

You can have everything in life that you want if you will just help enough other people get what they want. —Zig Ziglar

Unfortunately, one of the groups that didn't make the cut was Comfort Zone Camp. This really bothered me. I didn't start my own business to then be unable to invest in and support the causes I wanted. I guess I could have always overridden the decision, but it would have jeopardized jobs and future growth to make the donation. But I felt like I was letting down people I cared about, children who were counting on me and my company. After many restless nights, I was determined to find a way to help the camp, even if writing a company check was out of the question. I held a meeting with my team, and we discussed the dilemma. Fortunately, we were all on the same page and committed to finding a way to help. We decided the company would buy twenty-five entries in the name of Comfort Zone Camp for the Monument Avenue 10k, one of the nation's largest races and a hometown favorite.

A Run to Remember

A weight was lifted.

By leveraging a smaller initial investment, we could still raise money to support the camp. Race entries were offered to employees, clients, customers, and friends who were willing to pledge and raise money for the cause. To our great delight (and relief), the fundraiser took off. An IT director at a local company even volunteered to coach anyone who needed help training for the run. To emphasize the goal and create a real team spirit, we wore race shirts that read, "Capital TechSearch Runs for Comfort Zone Camp." Participation was completely optional, but with our spirits running high, the only two employees who didn't compete were out of town the weekend of the race with prior commitments.

In the end, we had a great time running with friends, clients, and coworkers, and we were able to donate more money than we had during our most profitable years. We started the fundraiser by investing less than half of what we would normally have donated, but then were able to give 60 percent more money than we had ever been able to give in the past. Not only were we able to continue helping Comfort Zone Camp, we reinforced the company's greater purpose of helping our community. We all worked together to complete a goal that was healthful, philanthropic, locally focused, and fun. What began as a simple donation to a good cause ultimately became a unifying force that built our team's strength and camaraderie in unexpected ways.

We started our foundation because we believe we have a real opportunity to help advance equity around the world...to help make sure that, no matter where a person is born, he or she has the chance to live a healthy, productive life. —Melinda Gates

On top of that, we created a spirit of giving and teamwork unmatched by any of our company's previous activities. We got to know our clients with an intimacy that only running together can foster. Our employees became involved in our company donations in ways that writing a check can never inspire. Best of all, we created a new tradition. Rallying together to support a good cause allowed us to rally around each other as well. We learned that even in the midst of financial turmoil, there's no real limit to how much you can help. Sometimes it just takes a little creativity.

Develop a Greater Purpose

Success means looking beyond the bottom line. Community involvement is about more than tax write-offs. Your company will reap greater rewards than anything you give: morale, teamwork, selfless service, world and community awareness, an antidote to stinky attitudes, a can-do spirit, belief in doing the right thing, self and corporate discipline—the list goes on and on.

Does money feel too tight? You can still make a significant impact in your community when you leverage more than just your checkbook.

When it comes to helping out, I don't believe in doing it for the media attention. My goal is to support the organizations that need help. —Paul Allen

Build your company's philanthropic focus and identity within your local community, and do everything in your power to support those causes. Don't dismiss the opportunity to give based on your revenue. If you approach the process with respect and care, then committing to causes—regardless of your profit and loss—can become the center of your company's greater purpose.

When you identify a worthy cause, get everyone involved. Employees develop a sense of ownership in their company's values when they actively participate in upholding them. That's more than writing a check can ever do. And employees often begin to work for more than a paycheck when they truly believe their company is built on strong ethics. One idea can open a new chapter for your company and community if you take the time to discover what you care about and act on it creatively.

He was the richest man in town, but he had lost the love of his life and had no friends. He was the object of ridicule, even by family members. Now that's a sad bedtime story. Luckily for Ebenezer Scrooge—and Tiny Tim Cratchit—some late-night visitors helped him experience a change of heart. As CEO, you have to watch your bottom line like a hawk, but it doesn't mean you have to say, "Bah! Humbug," to the people in need in your community.

The Moral of the Story

You must be profitable to stay in business. As a start-up CEO, your numbers are usually tight. But just like personal finances, generosity often adds more—purpose, faith, participation in the common good—than it subtracts.

For Reflection and Action

1. How important is your company to your community?

2. Who drives community involvement within your company? Are you aware of anyone in your company who is actively involved with a nonprofit?

3. What are some local organizations that could benefit from your company's contributions?

4. What are some benefits of community involvement, both on a personal level and for your company as a whole?

5. How do you envision your company's place within the community in ten years?

Chapter 12

DON'T HIRE AND FIRE HAPHAZARDLY

Hiring people is an art, not a science, and résumés can't tell you whether someone will fit into a company's culture. When you realize you've made a mistake, you need to cut your losses and move on.

—Howard Schultz

SOMETIMES IT'S BEST TO LET the Wizard hold on to the heart for a while and just rely on brains and courage. Like nearly everyone else, I started my company with people I felt comfortable around. One of my first hires was someone I'd known for twenty years. He had industry knowledge in a market where I was inexperienced. He worked for three fantastic weeks, accomplishing everything I'd hoped for and more. Then, like a prank that is supposed to be funny but ends up hurting property or person, he accepted a position with a larger, more established company. He had started feeling anxious about the risk involved in working for a start-up company. Honestly, I can't blame him. I was feeling anxious, too. My friend was gone, and I had just signed an office lease to accommodate both of us—space that I no longer needed, nor could I afford. Worse, I had client commitments that I no longer knew how to fulfill. My friend's tenure was short, but left a lasting impression on me as a business owner.

Looking back, I realize that initially, the only people I hired were friends. Some needed a job, but the crux of the matter was that I wanted the comfort of starting this journey with people I knew. I really felt some fit the bill, but in the end, none of them worked out. Zero. Surprisingly, I did not lose any close friends through this trial and error. I did, however, lose a lot of sleep.

The Art of Hiring and Firing

I have built a company culture that revolves around the people who work here, who share a dedication to one another and look after each other. I've purposely fostered this camaraderie because positive team environments bring purpose, direction, and synergy to accomplishing any chosen goal. This kind of collaborative and team-oriented culture would be destroyed by seemingly arbitrary or petty firings.

Your success as a start-up entrepreneur will be determined, in large measure, by how well you hire and fire. Some people are incredibly easy to fire. For whatever reason, their performance, attitude, or behavior—or some combination of all three—is so bad you wish you could erase them from your memory. They are a cancer to your company, and you have to cut them out. Gladly.

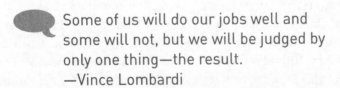

Some of us will do our jobs well and some will not, but we will be judged by only one thing—the result.
—Vince Lombardi

Then there are the employees who are hard to let go. They're the ones you really like. They might have families, but for whatever reason, they just can't cut it professionally. Their performance is poor. There is little to no chance of their excelling at their work. You know they need to go, but because you like them so much, it's hard to do what's best for your business.

It's natural to hire people you have a relationship with. Just be aware that the difficulty in terminating them is directly proportionate to how much you care for them. Personal relationships can get in the way of doing the right thing. You feel like a bad guy. Guilt and doubt cloud and delay the situation. You have measurable data to show why an employee isn't working out, but your heart says to try a little longer. A series of events in my company helped me realize I had to figure out how to lessen the mental anguish created by terminating someone. And no, it didn't involve learning not to care.

I had developed an especially close personal relationship with one of my employees. We were buds. It wasn't uncommon for us to head out for happy hour after work. His girlfriend would join us—and yes, she was as nice as could be too. We would hang out and blow off steam at organized company functions—Christmas parties, bowling after quarterly reviews, and so on. Here was a guy I truly felt was a great person. I enjoyed his company, and I liked being around him. He had a winning personality. On the surface, he seemed like the kind of employee I wanted to keep with the company for as long as possible.

But no matter how much I enjoyed his friendship, I could never shrug off one very important fact: He was not getting the job done. It seemed that all the after-hours bonding and office-hours encouragement in the world wasn't going to improve his lackluster professional performance. I really liked the guy and valued his friendship, but he consistently proved he wasn't going to help the company grow. In fact, if I didn't act on his mediocre performance, he was going to hold us back through his own work, and the message it sent to others would be: The boss has favorites who are held to different standards. Deep down I knew the time would soon come when I'd have to face the inevitable.

Executives owe it to the organization and to their fellow workers not to tolerate nonperforming individuals in important jobs. —Peter Drucker

From a professional standpoint, I recognized he really wasn't chopped liver. He just belonged somewhere else. Our high-octane, intense, and results-oriented environment was not right for him. Historically, we waited a minimum of three to six months to perform a rigorous evaluation of an employee, a time-frame that corresponded with the learning curve in our industry. But the longer we employed him—and six months had long ago come and gone—the more our lost opportunities compiled by not hiring someone better suited to the position.

Cut the Tail off the Monkey—Once

From a personal standpoint, delaying the inevitable only worsened the emotional toll of what was coming. The problem was, I didn't know how to quantitatively justify why he wasn't right for the job. I felt personally responsible for his success—or lack thereof. After all, I was the one who had hired him. I worked to turn the situation around.

I coached him.

I took him out for dinner.

I invited him into my home.

I hinted he needed to do better, usually with humor.

My indecisiveness hung over me like a bad dream. I lay awake at night trying to figure out how to handle the situation. Not only was he my friend, but he had a lot of other friends in the company. He was a popular guy. Would his dismissal have an impact on morale throughout the organization? Would our carefully built culture of work-and-play relationships be undermined if I couldn't demonstrate convincingly why he had to be fired? I worried about him financially. Would he find another job quickly enough to make his rent? How would this affect his pending engagement? I felt personally responsible for this young man's well-being. In my mind, *he* hadn't failed—the organization and I had failed *him*. We put him in the wrong position, and now he would experience the consequences of my mistake.

My guilt thickened and wrapped around me, squeezing tightly. I knew I had to let him go. We had talked many times about his performance, but he kept telling me his dog still had hunt in him. Without a real method of measuring his performance, I gave him chance after chance, hoping something would click. After months of suffocating guilt, I finally reached a breaking point and sat down with him to discuss his future with the company. We quickly agreed that it just wasn't working and it was time for his dog to hunt elsewhere.

He was actually relieved. He knew he wasn't making it and couldn't understand how he had kept his job as long as he did. I was living with self-imposed guilt. He was living with dread. My warning and coaching were like cutting the tail off a monkey one inch at a time—instead of one sharp cut. Since every cut hurts the same, better to do it once.

From that point on, I knew I had to make sure this kind of excruciating, drawn-out dismissal never happened again.

The Myth of the "Good Guy Boss"

I met with my advisory board to discuss our growth plans and the factors that had prevented successful expansion in the past. As I listened to the conversation in the room, my once-hidden answer became evident. I realized my desire to be the "good guy boss" or the "buddy boss" was actually backfiring when an employee didn't work out. Languidly floating through my employee relationships, not consistently making the necessary tough decisions, didn't serve the company or the employees. The only way to eliminate most of the stress involved in letting someone go was to institutionalize our human resources procedures.

Looking back on the situation, perhaps I believed that being the owner of a company—and a nice, big-hearted guy to boot—I had special powers to motivate others, even those who didn't want to be motivated. By putting an official hiring and firing plan in place, I no longer allowed irrelevant factors to cloud my judgment. I immediately felt a sense of relief. We built a qualitative and quantitative system that traced the same steps that helped everyone on my advisory board build their own careers. Personality and affability still mattered, and I still strived to hire employees with whom I could connect on a friendly level. But what changed was that before a candidate started with us—or from a very early point in his or her time with us—we were able to quantify why that person may or may not be an appropriate match for us.

You Don't Get What You Expect—But What You Inspect

For every prospective in-house employee, we began by filing a precise job description. Additionally, several team members interviewed each candidate, and each interviewer independently completed a specific scorecard. We also began to religiously check references, including third parties. And we required a sign-off from the individual authorized to make the candidate a job offer. I suppose as boss, I can veto someone else's veto. But I haven't.

Once a candidate was hired, we established *in writing* a clear set of expectations. For example, we recently hired three new employees, and each received clearly defined goals, along with weekly performance targets. We then tracked their levels of effort to meet expectations. We did not micromanage, but we did rigorously inspect their progress. We had made a commitment to inspect what we expect. In case you're getting the impression I'm a hiring and firing machine, let me assure you, we have reasonable expectations for new employees. We don't require immediate financial production or results, but we absolutely expect new hires to turn in reports on time and complete specific assignments. All of that is spelled out quite clearly for them.

For example, we told these new employees we expected them to make fifty phone calls within a certain time frame. In reviewing their progress, the supervisor asked, "How many did you make?" It doesn't get much simpler than that. Gauging performance against a measurable control is just one indicator that can tell us a great deal about a person's motivation. By sitting down with employees every week, we are able to positively compare and reflect on the results of their performance reviews. If they didn't perform up to par, was it because we hadn't trained them properly? Did they know how to complete the task? Were their skills affecting their performance, or was it their attitude? If it was their attitude, could it be addressed and improved? Or was it a true reflection of who they are and how they are going to act?

 My main job was developing talent. I was a gardener providing water and other nourishment to our top 750 people. Of course, I had to pull out some weeds, too. —Jack Welch

With our plan in place, I now felt comfortable making assessments because we had concrete methods for measuring performance. Upon review, we realized two of our new employees blossomed within the boundaries of concrete expectations. Like a fence around a playground, they felt safe to go all the way to the edge of their territory, rather than worrying about a ball rolling into traffic. Boundaries foster comfort and a sense of ownership within a defined space for many people.

When reviewing the third employee, however, I was reminded of the dilemma of firing my friend, whose stress-inducing dismissal led to the creation of these standards in the first place. We all really liked the third employee, who was a referral from another person in the company. Unfortunately, he didn't seem interested in reaching his targets, and he failed to meet expectations almost every week of his tenure.

This time, however, I was able to act professionally and without guilt. By applying our new standards, it became quantitatively clear that we were not the right employer for this individual. When we sat down and discussed the difference between our stated hiring expectations and his actual performance, surprisingly, we were all in agreement—including him. He knew he belonged somewhere else. He thanked me and resigned. No more cutting the tail off a monkey one painful inch at a time.

You're Not for Everyone

Unlike the previous experience of firing a poor performer, his resignation was a relatively painless process for everyone involved. No hurt feelings. No lost sleep. He was relieved to be released from the demands of a growing company. All this was possible because we created a very specific application of our institutionalized HR process, one that was very clear to the employee and to me. Feelings aside, the process was fair, and everyone was able to see and agree on why tough decisions needed to be made.

Quite frankly, not everyone will like working for you, and their performance will probably reflect this dissatisfaction. Isn't there a fail-safe way to know that before hiring? Probably not. It's nearly impossible to understand all a position entails until you're in it. Sometimes it doesn't take long to realize a job is not for you, and that's okay. By creating clear job descriptions, we improved our hiring dramatically. But we weren't perfect. Measurable standards enabled us to reach a decision about an employee's fitness for the company within a five-week probationary period instead of fourteen months. Letting go of certain employees will never be easy—and that's the way it should be. But I know having a tangible system helps the company's bottom line, better rewards for other employees who are exerting maximum effort, and ultimately serves the employee facing dismissal. Let's be honest, most people don't want to stay in a job they don't like or can't perform. But many stick it out as long as possible in order to keep a paycheck. In the end, they are likely better off moving on to a more rewarding position elsewhere.

Ready, Fire, Aim?

Before you let someone go, ask yourself:

1. Did I accurately and clearly define the job?

2. Did I provide the tools to succeed?

3. Have I provided truly constructive, direct feedback on performance issues?

4. Do I have this person in the right spot for their skills and interests? Is there another spot in the company where they could succeed?

5. If this person truly needs to be let go, what could I have done better to see this coming in the interview process?

By concretely addressing our company's hiring and firing expectations, we eliminated long, drawn-out, emotionally taxing dismissals. We were able to enforce quick and fact-driven decisions with little to no sense from others that we played favorites or were capricious. More importantly, we became better hirers.

Your Ogre-Free Zone

Institutionalize hiring and firing policies.

Write it down.

Measure it.

Stick to it.

I know this sounds like a pain, particularly if you are in the early days of your start-up. But ignore this issue at your own risk. Messy turnover is one of those dynamics that sap the energy of your company. If you can't do it, then pay someone else to do it. Or buy a commercial software package. A standardized process is not about changing who you are and what your company represents; it's about supporting success by building a foundation for successful employment in your business. Your life and business will be better and easier if you do, and you'll suffer untold misery if you don't.

When the expectations, processes, and intricacies of your business are written down, you have the strength and ability to guide your decisions with logic and grow your company with reason, not emotion. By creating clarity, you allow people to excel. You reduce the pain associated with letting someone go who doesn't rise to the challenge. Everyone, from new employees to key executives, can relax and thrive in their roles when they understand explicit expectations and those expectations are monitored in a predictable way. You don't have to be an ogre, and you can keep your friends. But you have to make sure everyone knows what's expected of them.

The prince and Cinderella of bedtime story and Disney fame actually had it easy. Oh, there were obstacles, including magical spells and wicked in-laws that kept them apart for a time. But all they needed to check out to know their love was "happily ever after" was whether the slipper fit her foot. As a CEO of a maturing company, shoe size isn't enough to base the suitability of who you want to hire!

The Moral of the Story

How you hire and fire will impact the greatness and success of your company. Institute excellent processes for hiring and firing based on clearly established performance expectations.

For Reflection and Action

1. Have you ever hired a close friend? Were you able to evaluate him or her objectively?

2. Has your company institutionalized HR, specifically the hiring and firing processes?

3. Have you established clear, written, and defined performance goals for the positions in your company? Do your employees feel these goals really matter and understand that you will inspect them?

4. Do your employees believe your company's employment decisions are guided by integrity and unbiased leadership?

5. Think about your own pre-entrepreneurial career in terms of knowing what you needed to do to succeed. Have you created the same environment at your own company?

Chapter 13

DON'T IGNORE WORST-CASE SCENARIOS

*I learned to embrace risk, as long as it was well thought out
and, in a worst-case scenario, I'd still land on my feet.*

—Eli Broad

M Y FRIEND JOHN AND I were playing golf on a Friday afternoon. We had set the day aside and were definitely going to hit the links no matter what. I got there early to load up the cart with clubs, balls, sunscreen, beer, and towels. My shoes were shined. Nothing else to do but stretch and do some last-minute putting practice. I felt relaxed with the sun shining on my face.

John showed up about sixty seconds before our tee time, shoes untied, his shirt halfway in and halfway out. John is usually pretty put together, and it was obvious he was preoccupied and uptight. He put his first tee shot out of bounds and was so mad that he said he was just going to drop up by my ball. There went our gentleman's bet for the day. Now *I* was in a bad mood. He threw a club after his second tee shot and let out an expletive I'd never heard from him. This was not the easygoing John that I knew. After the second hole, I asked him if he wanted to call it quits and go home. I'm not sure if I was being compassionate or looking to spare myself from having an eagerly anticipated golf game ruined by a friend who was ranting and raving. He looked at me, grabbed a beer, and began to tell me a story about something that he was dealing with in his business.

Introducing a Big-Time Plan

For the first three years he was in business, he didn't offer health benefits. Not because he didn't want to or because he didn't think they were important. He fully respected how important it was to carry health insurance in a world where one slip and fall or one illness can put an individual in dire financial straits. But with eight employees, he wasn't eligible for a group plan, and individually rating people can have enormous and far-reaching financial implications. Even if he could have managed to offer benefits to his small group of people from day one, what if something catastrophic had happened to one individual and forced the rates up for everyone to a point he couldn't afford? He didn't want to put something on the table, only to pull it off if things tightened even a little.

 Only as a warrior can one withstand the path of knowledge. A warrior cannot complain or regret anything. His life is an endless challenge, and challenges cannot possibly be good or bad. Challenges are simply challenges.
—Carlos Castaneda

Even though there was still risk involved, at the three-year mark, he felt that if he was going to be taken seriously by top prospective employees, he needed to roll out a big-time plan. He felt it was the right thing to do, and that it was a strategic advantage in the employment market, as he was ready to start hiring additional people in a low unemployment market. He did a considerable amount of due diligence on the various options and overall decision and felt as though he found a plan that created the right balance of risk and reward. He again considered the financial implications of a dramatic rate increase and also the psychological implications for employees if he had to withdraw benefits if, for some reason, they reached cost-prohibitive levels. "Here today, gone tomorrow" was not a message he wanted to send to his employees. After careful deliberation and assurances from his service provider that the odds were in his favor, he introduced the big-time benefits. On a personal level, he felt that this was a sign that his company was growing up.

In December 2007, he rolled out a great benefits package: major medical PPO and a 401(k) with matching contributions to all employees. He even waived the typical waiting period. Everyone would be eligible for the full package from day one with the company. Compared to the industry standard, his terms were top shelf. He believed these perks truly set him apart from his peers. Shortly after day one, however, he experienced his first wake-up call that bad things can happen to good benefits.

As I listened to him talk between vicious cuts at the little white ball, his agitation dissipated, and he relaxed. By the seventh hole, the golf game turned into what it was supposed to be: a nice afternoon of outdoor recreation with a friend. I have to admit, however, I wasn't very happy with what this counseling session had done to my game since my first drive straight down the fairway. He continued his story calmly.

A new employee had come on board a couple of weeks ago but had inexplicably left during the afternoon of his first day without telling anyone why and did not come back. It became a little bit of an afternoon buzz that had turned into a joke by day's end. No one knew what had happened, so there were tongue-in-cheek accusations of just whose personality was so bad a new hire couldn't last a day.

The next day, John received an e-mail from his new hire. He didn't give me the details of the message, but it basically said, "Hello, I really like the job. I can't wait to get back over there!

Unfortunately, when I got to work on Monday, I got a call from my doctor. I had some tests before I started working for you, and it looks like I have cancer. I couldn't stay at work Monday because I was too upset. I need a few weeks off for treatment. I really look forward to coming back to work."

 Success is not built on success. It's built on failure. It's built on frustration. Sometimes it's built on catastrophe.
—Sumner Redstone

What had been a humorous office incident was no longer a laughing matter.

John's worst-case scenario was coming true within weeks after rolling out his benefits plan. Even with group rates, a disastrous diagnosis for one employee could wreak havoc on his expense line. Of course, that's exactly why he had health benefits in the first place. They are there to defray the high costs of illness. Having lost my mother to a long and courageous battle with cancer several years earlier, I totally understand the financial and emotional implications of cancer diagnosis and treatment. No one wishes it on anyone at any time.

He had to compartmentalize the emotional side of this situation from the business side. He had boasted about offering employees benefits from the beginning. But now John had to define "beginning." In fact, he had to answer a slew of questions.

Most questions were directly related to this employee. Was this gentleman really eligible for benefits after six hours on the job? Had he filled out his paperwork and submitted it properly? Did this situation fall under that dark and cavernous umbrella known as the Family Medical Leave Act or the Americans with Disabilities Act?

Other questions were related more to his business. John had specifically hired the person to work with a high-profile client of his. What if the client, upon learning that the assigned employee could be out of the office for weeks at a time for treatment, didn't want this particular person on the job at all because the ramp-up time would increase? The new employee had a specific job to do within a specific time frame. What about the deadline? Was he going to have to add yet another salary to retain a good client?

A False Alarm or a Real Alarm?

We finished the conversation on the nineteenth hole. Golf was a mere afterthought. It turned out that John had an outstanding lawyer who had extensive experience in the area of health benefits for employees. He knew John's business, and they worked through a carefully orchestrated process to assess John's liability—and do the right thing. John's an ethical guy. Many attempts were made to contact the employee by registered letter, first informing him that he would be given all appropriate consideration and support to deal with his medical condition, but, secondly, that he needed to gather all pertinent diagnosis history and treatment protocols so the company could take the appropriate steps to provide the medical coverage he required.

There were irregularities on both his employment and medical applications and a question on the timing of the diagnosis. The situation looked potentially better for John financially—but the situation was still eating him up. Did this guy really have cancer? If so, was he okay?

Ever notice how your senses are
heightened when you are in challenging
situations? You're experiencing
an adrenaline rush that gives you
extra energy. If you see every day
as a challenge, you'd be surprised
how efficient you can become, and
how much can be accomplished.
—Donald Trump

Bottom line: John wanted to do the right thing for his employees. He had carefully thought through the possibilities. His worst-case scenario appeared and then disappeared in a short period of time. This kind of stuff—wacky, tragic, strange-but-true—happens every day, and as a business owner, you have to follow the proper steps, no matter how painful or messy, to set things straight on questions of liability. Fortunately, John had an established relationship with a trusted attorney who guided him through the situation.

Emergency Disaster Procedures

No matter how much thought or planning you put into establishing a safer, employee-friendly environment, sometimes *stuff* happens that you cannot anticipate. (I don't have to remind you what the coarse bumper sticker says). I think that is one of the core competencies of a successful entrepreneur—the willingness to deal thoughtfully and thoroughly with the unexpected. You never know what you are going to walk into on a particular day, but it is your responsibility, as the business owner and as the one with everything at risk, to solve anything that comes up.

As a start-up employer—particularly as one who is trying to do good by offering a top-rate benefits package myself—I can't help but feel a sense of unbounded liability toward my employees and clients. The sleepless-night kind of fear. One way I quiet the what-ifs that keep me awake is by retaining and using talented legal counsel that acts consistently, legally, ethically, and in *everyone's* best interest—not just my company's. This is not a time for you to skimp on legal fees and advice to improve your margin. The wrong decision or path of action in a time of crisis can put you out of business. If you just do the right thing all of the time (or try your best to do so), you will build up enough good karma to carry you through, right? Not necessarily.

Now is a good time to remind you again of the importance of establishing a professional support network. I know it is impossible to prepare for every eventuality, but the trusted, paid advisors you chose after reading chapter two could mean the difference between insomnia and a good night's sleep. Even if you have a law degree, the situations entrepreneurs encounter can be very specialized, and your business's future could depend on your ability to tap trusted advisors for their particular expertise.

One small town had a very effective emergency disaster system put in place. If a wolf threatened their flock of sheep, the young boy charged with tending them would simply cry, "Wolf!" at the top of his lungs and the townspeople would run to save him and their sheep. Seemed simple enough.

But the townsfolk discovered a few glitches in the system, particularly with a shepherd boy who was starved for attention. I'm sure you remember the tragic end to that tale—relying on one young boy didn't work out too well for the town or the boy. So the story really serves as a reminder that you, the CEO, should line up a battle plan for when things go wrong—but that you'd better remain vigilant yourself!

The Moral of the Story

As a start-up CEO, you can plan all you want and look at every contingency, but sometimes major calamities hit. Don't live in fear and worry, but be prepared for "disasters."

For Action and Reflection

1. If confronted with an unexpected situation with the potential to sink your company, who would you call for legal advice? Who would you call for business advice?

2. Do these people know your business, or will you spend the first three or four hours explaining who you are and what you do?

3. You can't anticipate every possible scenario that could disrupt your company, but do you have advisors with a depth of experience who could help prepare you for challenges and offer solutions when you face them?

4. Do you have competent administrators of your benefits packages? The details change constantly, as does the law. Who's keeping on top of that for you?

5. How do you keep your employees informed about any changes in their benefits?

Chapter 14

DON'T MESS AROUND WITH ROTTEN ATTITUDES

People are definitely a company's greatest asset. It doesn't make any difference whether the product is cars or cosmetics. A company is only as good as the people it keeps.

—Mary Kay Ash

W HAT DO YOU DO WHEN a top performer is tearing your team apart? At the Inc. 5000 conference last year, I had just left the last presentation of the day and was waiting to meet a friend to discuss some of the great ideas that we had heard throughout the day. These types of conferences are valuable for what you learn in workshops, but maybe even more for the networking. As I was waiting for him in a lobby chair, a woman I recognized from several workshops sat down and introduced herself as Kim. She was waiting for a group she was going to dinner with, so we killed some time talking.

Kim owned a disaster recovery company out of Seattle. We debated about which presentation was the best, and then the conversation shifted to our businesses. When I explained my sales background to her, she suddenly started laughing. I, of course, wanted to know what was so funny. She told me that several months earlier, she had fired her top salesperson. I didn't find that quite as funny as she did, but I asked her what went wrong. Was he too expensive? Why would anyone choose to get rid of a rainmaker? What she shared with me made the next twenty-five minutes much more valuable than "killing time."

The Ace Was an Ass

Her top rep was named Tom, and he was hitting his numbers out of the ballpark. Not only was he the highest-paid rep, but he was also the most profitable. Unfortunately, Tom wasn't a team player. Okay. Does that matter? As entrepreneurs, aren't we focused on results more than personalities? I hope so! I held off sharing these thoughts with her, and I'm glad I did. It may have shut down the conversation.

 Misery is a communicable disease.
—Martha Graham

Apparently, Tom chose not to socialize with anyone from the company. No big deal. He also didn't get along with the inside sales team who supported him by delivering leads to him. Maybe they were jealous. But he didn't stop there. He also mumbled nasty comments to and about everyone, and was generally miserable to be around. But he did deliver at a time when the rest of Kim's sales team was performing poorly. He'd been with the company for a few years and helped them stay afloat during a tough time. I asked if that wasn't enough to keep him. She shook her head and said that now he created more drama than he was worth. He affected productivity by the way he disrespected other employees.

Put yourself in Kim's shoes. What would you do with someone causing problems on a personal level, but contributing from a financial standpoint? Tom was making money for the company but was also acting like a complete jackass. Would you fire him?

Tom was right out of college and very smart, but he had been relatively unprofessional from day one. He expressed a sense of entitlement and a singular dedication to his own success—with zero concern for anyone else's—that made it impossible for him to fit in as a true team player. In current conditions, she said, he would not have made it a month in her company as a new hire. But when she first hired him, Kim ran a pretty loose ship. Tom didn't have a defined chain of command, and no one really watched over him. With much of the company's energy focused on making payroll, this top performer's lousy attitude seemed like the least of Kim's problems.

And Tom's boorish behavior had gotten worse.

When Kim hired someone else from the outside to improve company processes, his already unpleasant manner deteriorated even further. He got to the point where he would only work on the things that were easy or of interest to him, and had stopped traveling to all his accounts. He was living off of a revenue and commission stream that he had built over the previous years and was just doing the minimum to get by.

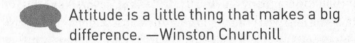 Attitude is a little thing that makes a big difference. —Winston Churchill

When he decided—in the heart of the fourth-quarter push and despite Kim asking him not to—that it would be a good time to take a vacation for several weeks to tour the Grand Canyon, he was skating on thinner ice than he realized. Kim said if he was going to go anyway, she hoped some rest and relaxation would improve his outlook and behavior—for his own good. But he picked up right where he left off when he came back. He came in with his head down, making "yeah, whatever" comments under his breath in response to anything said to him. Kim pulled him aside for one last effort to determine what was going on with him and to see if there was a way to work things out.

He wouldn't answer any of her questions directly. He just mumbled that his sales were fine, so what did it matter how he treated his teammates? She honestly didn't know how this guy could even sell. It was a mystery. He always made his numbers. She was about to let things slide again, even after he was rude to her. Bottom line: She needed his revenue stream. But then she took a walk around her office and didn't recognize the joyful place she used to run. People looked at her suspiciously. "Heck," she said, "why not? I wasn't having any fun either. This jackass was ruining my life." So she drew a line in the sand right then and there. She called him back into her office and told him to clean out his desk. His attitude was not going to turn around, and his sales savvy was no longer worth it.

Blocking the Sunshine

As she discussed the situation with her management team that afternoon, Kim realized that no single person is more important than the company and the whole team. She knew she did the right thing and was ready to accept the consequences. She knew people would be relieved with Tom gone, but wondered if they would be as nervous as she was to lose his revenue stream.

When she announced Tom's departure to the whole team the next morning, she was taken aback at how quickly the general mood had lightened. No one broke into song the second they heard Tom was gone. But almost as quick as the first blare of a horn when the light turns green in New York City, people were laughing and joking with each other again. There was no more tiptoeing around a world-class grouch. By the next quarter, the financial effect was almost as instantaneous. Employees who had been hesitant began stepping up and delivering. In short, everyone started performing better, and productivity went through the roof. Kim had been thinking Tom was the only bright spot in her struggling company, but he was really the one giant dark cloud that had been blocking the sun.

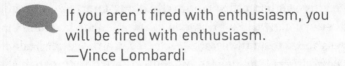

If you aren't fired with enthusiasm, you
will be fired with enthusiasm.
—Vince Lombardi

Under easier circumstances, without the distractions of the economic environment she was dealing with, she would have noticed Tom's behavior and let him go much sooner. Nonetheless, the instant upswing after his departure reminded her of a crucial lesson that in any organization, one person has a greater ability to *negatively* impact progress than to *positively* drive it. Kim had been working for months to resolve the company's financial problems, believing Tom was one of the only saving graces keeping her in the black. By letting his behavior slide, she learned that sometimes you might be focusing on symptoms when you should determine the underlying cause of an ailment. His attitude had become like a virus, infecting everything and everyone around him. Including her.

As if the company's turnaround wasn't enough proof that Tom's departure was a good thing, an employee came forward later and said he discovered a negative comment Tom had written about him in the company's master database. After witnessing the simultaneous change in morale and revenue after Tom left, Kim analyzed why she'd let his cancerous behavior slide and how she might deal with similar problems more directly in the future.

Don't Let One Person Set the Wrong Tone

Why a whole chapter on cutting loose difficult people? Didn't we cover this in the hiring and firing chapter? Yes and no. An abusive top performer represents a different challenge—and temptation. It's not that you don't want to fire them because you like them. But you may be tempted to feel like you can't live without them.

One person's bad attitude, disrespect, or otherwise intolerable behavior can be like quicksand to any company, sucking the life out of other employees and bringing down overall performance. We're not talking about perfection. People can have a bad day. Some are more social than others. Talented people can be quirky. You can be tolerant and affirming, but when you keep hearing little things from multiple people about the same person, you need to become vigilant and pay attention to what your employees are saying.

Don't sweep your findings under the rug. If you have a good performer whose presence is negatively affecting others, the person is probably impeding every other person's ability to succeed. Get to the bottom of the behavior issues, and then dig ten feet below that to find out what's driving the negativity. It's impossible to give a job everything you've got if you don't believe in what you're doing.

What's the answer? Eat, sleep, and breathe consistency. If you tolerate unacceptable behavior from anyone, even a top performer, you are setting the company up for a whole host of multiplied problems. Letting one person or team get away with selfish or damaging acts makes every other employee lose faith in the company. At a minimum, the inequality makes their jobs harder. If you allow someone or some group to repeatedly challenge others in a negative way, your productivity and profit will suffer. From the outside, it may look like the tough employee is your best employee, but that may be because he is dragging everyone else down.

Again, argument and strongly held views are necessary. Your business isn't a church picnic. But a threshold is crossed when a person's attacks become personal on a regular or chronic basis. Conflict and hurt feelings can be handled with apologies and a handshake. A pattern of peer abuse isn't forgiven so easily. The needs of an individual or a small team do not come before the overall mission of the entire enterprise.

When patterns emerge, you need to be more like a detective than an ostrich. Make sure you get the facts straight, and don't think that by ignoring them they'll go away. Employees need to know what is expected of them, and they need to know they are working in a safe, fair environment.

 Businesses are made by people. We've proven time and time again that you can have wonderful shop, and put a bloke in there who's no good, and he'll stuff it up. Put a good bloke in, and it just turns around like that. —Gerry Harvey

It was a time of enlightenment. A brutal, superstitious island in the sea, made up of warring clans and tribes, was uniting as a nation. No longer would might make right—but right would make right. No longer would the people live under the whims and furies of a tyrant, but this new king would share power and pursue justice and peace. King Arthur fashioned a round table to symbolically show this new day of dialogue. Now that's what I call a bedtime story!

But Camelot was a vapor. Short-lived. Broken apart by war. It wasn't undone by a small and petty man, but by the greatest knight of the realm, Sir Lancelot. The very man who fought valiantly beside Arthur to unite the kingdom had let his self-preoccupation and lusts tear it apart. He slept with the king's wife. Arthur's sin was that he let it happen.

As CEO, your conference room may not have a round table, but you are still charged with holding your kingdom together!

The Moral of the Story

Attitudes, over time, will outperform ability. Don't let a destructive person, even if talented, ruin the morale of your company.

For Action and Reflection

1. Have you ever overlooked a personnel problem, and instead of going away, it turned into a monster?

2. Think about your own team. Do any of your employees consistently bring the others down? How? Why?

3. What is the potential impact of one overly negative employee?

4. Do you have processes in place to guard against a bad hire? To help you address a previous bad hire?

5. Do your employees feel comfortable coming to you about sensitive issues? If there's a "Tom" in your office, is somebody going to let you know what's really going on?

Chapter 15

DON'T TOLERATE SLOPPY AND OFF-COLOR COMMUNICATION

> It takes twenty years to build a reputation and five minutes
> to ruin it. If you think about that, you'll do things differently.
> —Warren Buffett

NEW TECHNOLOGIES STREAMLINE A RICH communication environment. E-mail, social networking, Twitter, search engines, and image and video hosting are all great, but they create potential liabilities for you and your business.

What would happen if one of your employees composed an offensive memo, printed it on company letterhead, and mailed it to fifty people inside and outside the office? That would be embarrassing and damaging. Now, what if the same thing happened, but rather than circulating a memo on company letterhead, the communication was a rude joke forwarded to the same fifty people using company e-mail? Gut instinct might tell you the first example is more egregious than the second, but the liability is exactly the same: inflammatory, possibly illegal, traceable communication with your company's name forever attached.

Faster Isn't *Always* Better

Computers and the Internet have permanently changed the world of business. Everything happens faster: communication, file sharing, data collection, marketing, design, and more. But while streamlined processes are usually a good thing, instant communication offers the same hazards as speaking before thinking: Without the filter of time or contemplation, it's easy to unwittingly say or write something offensive or even illegal.

 With "multimedia" the profound ethical and aesthetic challenge comes from the burden of responsibility that lies with the individual once the constraints on communications are so radically eased if not eliminated.
—Kenneth Dyson

Traditionally, business letters are composed with deliberation and attention to detail. E-mails, however, are usually fired off at the hint of a thought or idea. Informal and immediate, it's easy to dismiss the impact of e-mails that include off-color comments, inane forwards, or sloppy grammar. People have come to expect and accept the lax and casual tone of electronic communication, even in business settings, and more lenient standards have evolved for employees—a legally risky phenomenon. According to Deborah H. Juhnke, vice president of Computer Forensics Inc., "E-mail is a highly valuable source of evidence in sexual harassment cases, antitrust cases, and other cases where casual communication takes on the mantle of corporate policy" ("What Lies Beneath: Reducing Exposure in Litigation," in *Litigation and Support in the Information Age*, June 2001).

As a business owner, I've always expected my employees to conduct themselves professionally, and for the most part, they do. Now, I know no one is perfect and everyone makes mistakes—myself included—but when it comes to electronic communication, I have been shocked by some of the stories I have heard about employee behavior, from insults over instant messaging to inappropriate comments in e-mails. For some, all logic seems to disappear when virtual communication is involved.

A friend who owns a company that provides services to assisted living facilities sent me an e-mail late one afternoon to see if we could meet for a cup of coffee. We had provided each other with some mutual advice as fellow entrepreneurs, and I always got something out of our talks. I met him in a brightly lit atrium lounge on a beautiful summer evening but one look at him, and you could almost see the sky grow dark with the storm clouding his face!

He was in no mood for chit-chat and immediately hit what was on his mind. One of his employees alerted him to a rude comment posted about that employee on their intranet, which was accessible and used by everyone in the company. Initially, my friend was simply curious to read the note. Upon opening it, however, his curiosity immediately turned to disbelief. The comment, written by a former employee, was downright offensive. He knew the note's author and was pretty sure it was originally intended as a joke—but not a joke for public consumption. Unlike verbal teasing, a person's tone of voice is nearly impossible to decipher on a computer screen. Taken out of context, the note was blatantly insulting, if not a form of harassment. But even if it had been clearly labeled as a joke, posting it reflected incredibly poor judgment. Disappointed, he immediately erased the message and apologized to the concerned employee.

Because his company's intranet was easy to use and held a huge amount of vital data, it was a busy site, and he felt incredibly thankful no one else discovered the virtual slam (as far as he knew). But, though the whistle-blower was satisfied with his actions, my friend was left with a lingering feeling this was not an isolated incident. On a hunch, he went back into the database and searched for every curse word he could come up with, from minor to major vulgarity. Much to his dismay, he found quite a few examples that would have been damaging to the company.

He felt as though he had let his people down because he hadn't policed the data.

Unfortunately, the database debacle wasn't the only time something of this caliber had happened to him. Before this last event, one incident led to the removal of instant messenger from all company computers, and another incident resulted in an employee making a forced apology to the entire company during one of his meetings. He had been slow to measure how pervasive a problem this was.

The level of immaturity and liability was enough to make him feel like he was the principal of a middle school rather than the president of a professional company.

He felt betrayed. He understood that the younger generation's approach to electronic communication was more relaxed. They grew up communicating with their friends electronically. Even so, he was running a business. He had to rein in the company's communications.

After going through the disgusting quality and quantity of database comments, creating and enforcing a new communication policy immediately became one of his most important focuses. He always had such a policy, but it was not sufficiently broad, strict, discussed, or enforced. I knew he was picky about hiring people. His application process was more rigorous than mine and I thought was near guilty of overkill at times. After this incident, though, he implemented a new, stricter policy that was included in his employment agreement. He told me that every one of his employees was not only required to sign a communication agreement, but he had implemented processes to make sure they heeded it. Frequent, systematic database checks were developed by an IT consultant so bad behavior wouldn't slip through the cracks. Additionally, he brought in a communications expert to discuss e-mail etiquette and professionalism in an all-company seminar. He said this would happen annually. He was obviously serious about raising the professionalism that he believed his company should exhibit. The offenses stopped almost immediately with his renewed focus. Now everyone knew what happened if damning evidence was uncovered: immediate dismissal. Zero tolerance. Wow. I knew he was right to make this a priority, but I wasn't sure I was ready to go that far. No matter— the important thing was to start somewhere.

Don't Say It

Don't say it—or send it—if the remark...

- Puts down a person or group of persons on the basis of race, sex, age, or creed.
- Finds humor in the crude or profane.
- Makes light of a tragedy.
- Declares there is a right or wrong political party or view.
- Would cause customers to question your judgment.
- Is something you wouldn't want your mom or your spouse or your kids to hear from you.

I thought his approach sounded a bit paranoid and harsh, and we argued that point back and forth, but this was a face-to-face meeting where he really wasn't looking for feedback as much as he was testing his own instincts out loud. He felt good about where he landed. I had to agree, it wasn't smart for him— or me—to expose our employees, our businesses, our families, and ultimately our own reputations to irreparable harm due to someone's locker-room humor or vulgar insults. I followed his approach with the zero tolerance component.

Protect Your Brand

No one wants to police a person's private life. But your company server isn't private. Yet, people feel free to hit porn sites, do their Christmas shopping, read restaurant reviews, stay in touch with the thousand of their friends on Facebook, and do other activities not acceptable for the work environment. You may not want to feel like a spy, but you should check your databases. Make sure every employee understands and abides by your communication policy. And if you don't have one yet, write it or pay someone to write it now. Along with profitability and growth, protecting your company's brand and reputation should rank as one of your most important priorities. An employee's offhand comment or tasteless e-mail may be a one-time mistake, but it's crucial that you know what's circulating with your company's name attached. Your livelihood, reputation, and money are on the line, always.

As a sports fan, I can't go without a nod to this genre as one of my bedtime stories. And I won't just reference one story but several that make the same point: All the good we accomplish can be lost by one single event! How about Barry Bonds, Alex Rodriguez, and Roger Clemens? Will they be remembered for their homerun and pitching prowess—or accusations of steroids? Is tennis legend John McEnroe remembered more for his on-court artistry with a racquet or his public tirades and tantrums?

As a CEO building a brand, don't let sloppy and inappropriate communication sully all you have accomplished!

The Moral of the Story

You can spend your whole life building an outstanding personal and professional reputation, only to have it torpedoed by some inappropriate remark.

For Reflection and Action

1. Do you know what's lurking in your company's database? It could bite you.

2. Do you have a written policy for electronic communication? Is every employee aware of it?

3. How lax are you when it comes to your own electronic communications? Do you send or forward questionable e-mails from work?

4. Do you openly discuss proper etiquette and composition of company e-mails? Do you recognize the generation gap with younger employees when it comes to electronic communication, and do they understand your expectations as a business owner?

5. Are your employees clearly aware of the consequences of sending or saving libelous or questionable messages?

NOTHING LIKE A GOOD NIGHT'S SLEEP

I HOPE I HAVEN'T GIVEN ANYONE considering, or already pursuing, the entrepreneurial path a bad case of insomnia. I know I've shared some stories that can be more than a little scary when you and your livelihood are on the line. A proper sense of respect—and yes, fear—is not a bad starting point in creating your enterprise.

But I hope that I have communicated even more strongly my belief in, and passion and joy for, the adventure of being an entrepreneur. Starting a new company is a wonderful experience. It is good for our country, but even better at bringing out the best in us.

I haven't hit every issue involved in a start-up, and I certainly didn't set out to provide an exhaustive blueprint or checklist of what you need to be successful. What I really wanted to provide you with is the feeling you get when you talk to a good friend. That friend listens and shares and helps you. Even if he doesn't have all the answers. Good friends are encouragers who help us accomplish things we didn't know we could pull off.

One last bedtime story.

She was the best friend he ever had. Truth be told, she was in love with him and secretly harbored the longing that he would love her in the same way. She wanted to be more than a friend. Alas, his heart was always looking elsewhere. Still they had tremendous fun and perilous adventures together, always at one another's side. Forever there to support and protect. But one day she did something that angered him, and he declared their friendship null and void. He wasn't as perceptive as she and didn't realize that his words and actions were her death sentence. Without Peter to believe in her, Tinkerbell would cease to exist.

But we know how the story ends. Peter does believe in her—and asks the audience to do the same by clapping for her—and she comes back to life, brighter and perkier than ever.

You have people who believe in you. Maybe, when you get too busy and preoccupied, you can't hear them clapping. But they're there for you. In fact, this book is my way of cheering you on and saying you can do it.

Your new enterprise will still be filled with sword fights and a time or two when you think you might be walking the plank. But with the support and confidence of others behind you, you can soar—and get a good night's sleep along the way.

ABOUT THE AUTHOR

DAVID INGRAM IS THE FOUNDER, president, and CEO of Capital TechSearch, headquartered in Richmond, Virginia. He has a deep understanding of—and great empathy for—the business challenges that his fellow entrepreneurs face.

After its founding in 2001 as an executive search firm, Capital TechSearch expanded in 2004 to provide staffing services to its clients in the information technology industry. Capital TechSearch provides support in business intelligence, data warehousing, database administration, Web development, infrastructure, and quality assurance. From 2004 to 2009, the company's revenues increased more than 436 percent, leading Capital TechSearch to be included on the prestigious Inc. 5000 list of the country's fastest-growing private companies in 2008 and 2009.

David got an early start in entrepreneurship. In high school, he created a landscaping company and borrowed enough capital to acquire a competitor. Before graduating from college and entering the corporate world, he had sold the combined companies for a profit.

With an extensive background in technical sales, sales management, and operations, David has worked for such well-known companies as Kana Communications (NASD: KANA), Noochee Solutions, Parametric Technology (NASD: PMTC), and Lanier Worldwide.

David currently sits on the Board of Directors for the Virginia Council of CEOs, a nonprofit dedicated to executive education and the sharing of information amongst peers. He has served as a guest lecturer for postgraduate classes at the University of Richmond Robins School of Business, the Virginia Commonwealth University School of Business, and the East Carolina University College of Business.

Nationally recognized for his insight into entrepreneurship, staffing, and executive hiring, David has been quoted in *Forbes.com, HR,* and *Certification* magazines. He is also a popular speaker for business events, and has served as an expert panelist for many local and national organizations, such as Altria and the American Staffing Association.

A native of the Northern Virginia area, David graduated from Hampden-Sydney College with a double degree in managerial economics and French. He lives in Richmond with his wife, Meridith; twin sons; and daughter. For more information, visit www.15bedtimestories.com or www.capitaltechsearch.com, e-mail dave@capitaltechsearch.com, or follow him on Twitter at www.twitter.com/bedtimestories.